THE ADVENT OF JESUS

A DEVOTIONAL CELEBRATING THE COMING
SAVIOR

HOLIDAY CELEBRATION DEVOTIONALS
BOOK 1

PETER DEHAAN

Library of Congress Control Number: 2022916010

Published by Rock Rooster Books, Grand Rapids, Michigan

ISBNs:

- 979-8-88809-003-9 (e-book)
- 979-8-88809-004-6 (paperback)
- 979-8-88809-005-3 (hardcover)
- 979-8-88809-022-0 (audiobook)

Credits:

- Developmental editor: Kathryn Wilmotte
- Copyeditor: Robyn Mulder
- Cover design: Taryn Nergaard
- Author photo: Chelsie Jensen Photography

To Michael Roberto for suggesting, not once, but several times, that I write this devotional

Series by Peter DeHaan

Holiday Celebration Devotionals rejoice in the holidays with Jesus.

40-Day Bible Study Series takes a fresh and practical look into Scripture, book by book.

Bible Character Sketches Series celebrates people in Scripture, from the well-known to the obscure.

Visiting Churches Series takes an in-person look at church practices and traditions to inform and inspire today's followers of Jesus.

Be the first to hear about Peter's new books and receive updates at PeterDeHaan.com/updates.

CONTENTS

CELEBRATING THE COMING OF JESUS

Most Christians and their churches celebrate Christmas to commemorate Jesus coming to earth as a baby. And many build up to Christmas by observing Advent—the time that precedes our Savior's birth.

This book is designed to guide us in this important season as we celebrate Jesus.

In doing so, we'll take a holistic approach so we can better appreciate the coming of our Savior to earth. We'll center on the gospel accounts in the Bible, giving primary attention to the beloved passage from the beginning of the book of Luke. Then we'll incorporate Old Testament prophecy about the coming Messiah to deepen our understanding. Along the way we'll tap into our imagination to better see things from the perspective of Mary and Joseph.

The goal is to consider Jesus's arrival from several different vantages to offer a comprehensive Advent devotional. And for maximum flexibility, there are options to fit your preferences and schedule. Here's why:

Traditionally, Advent begins on the fourth Sunday before Christmas.

As a result, Advent can start as early as November 27 or as late as December 3. This means that the length of Advent varies from 22 to 28 days.

It ends with the celebration of Jesus's birth on December 25, even though this date is one of convenience and probably does not mark Jesus's actual birth.

In this devotional we'll celebrate the arrival of Jesus for all twenty-eight days of Advent. You can start on November 27, regardless of the year's calendar. Or begin on whatever date marks the beginning of Advent for the current year.

We'll build up to the grand culmination of Jesus's birth.

Then, if you want more, continue the celebration past Christmas to Epiphany on January 6, which traditionally marks the coming of the Magi to celebrate Jesus. This event serves as a fitting conclusion to the Christmas story.

To cover all the essential parts of the story, we'll compress some parts of our timeline and expand others. For example, we'll look at Jesus's birth for five days, not just on Christmas. And we'll do the same for Epiphany.

The result is a comprehensive devotional that celebrates Jesus coming to earth as an infant who grows up to save humanity. May God speak to you through this book during the Advent season and beyond.

NOVEMBER 27: IN THE BEGINNING

TODAY'S PASSAGE: JOHN 1:1–13

Focus verse: *In the beginning was the Word, and the Word was with God, and the Word was God.* (John 1:1)

L et's start at the beginning. Jesus's story doesn't open with his birth. It doesn't begin at the announcement of his conception. And it doesn't start with the Old Testament prophecies that foretell the coming Messiah. To start at the beginning, we must go back even further.

From our perspective, Jesus's story begins at creation, at the dawn of time. He was there. All things that were made, were made by him. This means that Jesus is not only our Savior, but also our Creator.

The apostle John's poetic biography of Jesus makes this clear. Without Jesus, we and the world we live in wouldn't exist.

John opens his epic book with the words "In the beginning." Interestingly, the opening passage in the Bible, from Genesis, also starts with this phrase: "In the beginning."

Yet in Genesis there's a fourth word: God. As in "In the beginning, God." Though in Genesis we might wonder if God refers to Father God or God as Trinity (Father, Son, and Holy Spirit), John confirms that Jesus *was* there and played an integral part in the formation of our reality. (And the Holy Spirit's presence is implied as well in Genesis 1:2.)

Whereas Genesis opens with "In the beginning, God," John opens with "In the beginning was the Word." This doesn't reference the written word of God (Scripture) or the spoken word of God (the Holy Spirit), but God himself. In actuality, Jesus is *the* Word of God.

As *the* Word of God—both Creator and Savior—Jesus embodies life. His life shines brightly in the darkness to all people so that they may believe and receive him. In doing so they become children of God. *We* may become children of God.

John establishes Jesus's presence at creation. Yet this is not his beginning either, but merely the earliest account where we see him at work. As eternal God, Jesus precedes our world as timeless and immortal, without beginning or end. He is everlasting, coming to us from infinity past and lasting with us into infinity future.

Yet despite all that he is, he condescends to humble himself and enter our physical reality as a helpless baby so that he may one day save us.

Questions: *Do we celebrate Jesus as both our Creator and our Savior? Have we received him and become children of God?* (See John 1:12–13.)

Prayer: Thank you, Jesus, for who you are and what you did. May we always remember this and to celebrate all that you've done for us—and are doing.

NOVEMBER 28: THE COMING OF JOHN THE BAPTIST

TODAY'S PASSAGE: MARK 1:1–3

Focus verse: *The beginning of the good news about Jesus the Messiah, the Son of God.* (Mark 1:1)

L ike the books of Genesis and John, which open with the phrase "In the beginning," Mark takes a similar approach. But he's more succinct, simply saying, "The beginning." This brevity seems appropriate, given that Mark's biography of Jesus is the shortest and most concise of the four.

Mark opens by making it clear what he's writing about. He wants to tell his audience about the beginning of the good news of Jesus, who comes into the world to save the world as their Messiah. He is the Son of God.

Mark confirms his premise by citing Old Testament prophecy. He names Isaiah as the writer of the passage he quotes. This is only partially correct: Malachi wrote the first part and Isaiah penned the second.

While we might want to criticize Mark for his lack of precision, it's unlikely he had a copy of the scroll of Isaiah's prophetic words to consult. Instead, he relied on his memory or the recollection of others who had memorized much of the Old Testament.

The point isn't that Mark only partially cites the source of his material. The more critical element is that he does correctly quote Scripture, albeit from two separate passages instead of one. Referencing two sources, however, strengthens the veracity of his teaching, with both Isaiah and Malachi standing in agreement about what is to come.

Contrary to what we might expect, however, these two separate passages aren't about Jesus. Instead, they're about John the Baptist, who will arrive on the scene before Jesus. Although only about six months older than Jesus, John will grow up to precede him and prepare the way for him.

John will facilitate Jesus's ministry by challenging people to think about what they've done wrong and point them to the Messiah as the solution to their shortcomings (their sins).

John will make the path to Jesus straight.

Questions: *If we had only our memory to rely upon, how much of the Bible would we know? What can we do to point people to Jesus?*

Prayer: Lord, show us and inspire us to hide your word in our heart (Psalm 119:11). Strengthen us to go out into the world and tell others about Jesus.

NOVEMBER 29: MALACHI'S PROPHECY: PREPARE THE WAY, PART 1

TODAY'S PASSAGE: MALACHI 2:17–3:5

Focus verse: *"I will send my messenger, who will prepare the way before me."* (Malachi 3:1)

The opening of Mark's gospel quotes two Old Testament prophecies about John the Baptist. The first is from Malachi, the final book in the Old Testament.

But Malachi isn't speaking his own words. He quotes directly from God, the Lord Almighty. In this way, we hear our Lord's own words through his prophet and servant Malachi.

God says he will one day send someone to go before him and prepare the way for him. The messenger, as we'll later learn, is John the Baptist. He will go ahead of Jesus to make the way for him.

Now let's pull back a bit and look at the prophet's words in context. To do so we'll need to start at Malachi 2:17 and read to Malachi 3:5.

Malachi writes that the people have wearied God with their words.

"How?" the people ask, not understanding their failings.

They do so by calling evil good (see Isaiah 5:20–21) and assuming God is pleased with them. They also question God's apparent lack of justice.

In response to these people who weary God with their twisting of words and insulting accusations, he shares his solution. He'll send a messenger tasked with preparing the way for *me* to come. And by *me*, he means Jesus.

After God's messenger makes the way, then Jesus will suddenly appear. He'll be the one they seek, the solution they desire.

"But who can endure his coming?" Malachi asks. "Who can stand before him?" These questions may seem like Jesus is someone we should fear. But we can also see this as a reason to revere God as the awesome Lord that he is.

In addition, Malachi writes that the message

will purify them and refine them to make them—and us—right before God.

He'll also speak out against sorcerers (false religions), adulterers (sexually immoral practices), and perjurers (liars). He will oppose those who cheat their workers, take advantage of widows and orphans, and prevent outsiders from receiving justice.

This is our Lord's response to the naysayers who ask, "Where is God's justice?"

Jesus will come to bring justice (see Luke 11:42 and Acts 17:31). Even more importantly, Jesus will provide a solution to make us right with Father God.

Questions: *In what ways might we weary God with our words? Do we care as much about justice as God does? Most significantly, have we allowed Jesus to make us right with his Father?*

Prayer: Jesus, may we have a heart aligned with yours for justice and then act to pursue it. May our actions to promote justice serve as both an act of worship and as a witness.

NOVEMBER 30: ISAIAH'S PROPHECY: PREPARE THE WAY, PART 2

TODAY'S PASSAGE: ISAIAH 40:3–4

Focus verse: *A voice of one calling: "In the wilderness prepare the way for the Lord."* (Isaiah 40:3)

The second passage Mark quotes in his biography of Jesus comes from Isaiah 40:3. This verse also foretells the coming of John the Baptist, who will make the way for the Lord, that is, Jesus.

John will be a voice calling to the people from the wilderness (the desert), which will prepare the way for Jesus to come. Jesus will straighten out the path to God, a highway to speed us right to him. To do so, every valley along the way must be raised and every mountain must be lowered. This will turn hilly terrain into a level road on a smooth plain.

In short, Jesus will make it easy for us to approach God. He will establish a new covenant for us.

This is quite a contrast to the covenant revealed in the Old Testament. The old way involved following rules, a mind-blowing number of them that detailed exacting expectations. The law of Moses lists 613 laws that God expected his people to obey. Some of these rules were actions to follow, and others were actions to avoid.

If this isn't overwhelming enough, well-meaning followers of God attempted to clarify exactly what these 613 laws meant. They expanded on the Torah, which resulted in the Talmud, with thousands of pages and tens of thousands of rules to guide righteous Jewish practice.

But without faith it's impossible to obey all these rules and thereby please God (Hebrews 11:6).

Whoever follows the law exactly as specified and stumbles over just one point is guilty of breaking it all (James 2:10).

This is why Jesus must come. He'll provide a new way to approach God, a better way. His way makes the path to God straight, leveling the mountains and valleys to make that highway.

We go down this path when we follow Jesus and become his disciple. Following hundreds or thousands of rules is hard. Saying yes to Jesus is easy.

Questions: *How many rules do we think we must follow to approach God and guide our relationship with him? Have we said yes to Jesus by following him and being his disciple?*

Prayer: Thank you, Jesus, for providing a better way to be made right with Father God. May we accept this in faith and push aside the idea that we must follow a list of rules to approach you.

DECEMBER 1: THE COMING OF JOHN THE BAPTIST

TODAY'S PASSAGE: LUKE 1:5–25

Focus verse: *"Do not be afraid, Zechariah; your prayer has been heard. Your wife Elizabeth will bear you a son, and you are to call him John."* (Luke 1:13)

W e've already covered how John and Mark begin their biographies of Jesus. Now we'll consider Luke's version. He starts with a story, the account of Zechariah and Elizabeth.

Zechariah is a priest, a descendant of Aaron. His wife, Elizabeth, is likewise from Aaron's line. Though they've been married a long time, they have no children. Luke says they are "very old."

One day, as Zechariah works in the temple, an

angel comes to him, startling the priest. The angel, Gabriel, tells Zechariah that God has heard his prayer and will give him and Elizabeth a son. Gabriel even tells Zechariah to name the boy John.

Not only will John be a delight to his parents, but many will celebrate his birth because he will be great in God's eyes. John is, therefore, to live a life set apart. He is not to drink wine or anything fermented. Instead, the Holy Spirit will fill him, even before his birth.

Gabriel then tells Zechariah what John will do when he grows up.

John will point people to God, bringing back many who have fallen away. He will precede the Lord (that is, Jesus).

Just like the prophet Elijah, John will move with the same spirit and power. John will restore right living, turning the hearts of the disobedient to seek the wisdom of righteousness.

He'll work to prepare the people to receive Jesus.

Even though Zechariah has been praying for a son, the priest is skeptical at the angel's promise. Because he doubts Gabriel's declaration, Zechariah will be unable to speak until the angel's words come true.

When the now-silent Zechariah's work at the temple is complete, he goes home. We can imagine it's a homecoming like none before, with increased anticipation over the angel Gabriel's unexpected, incredible words.

Elizabeth soon gets pregnant.

Questions: *What can we do to be like John and point people to Jesus? Are we willing to move in the spirit and power of Elijah?*

Prayer: God, we thank you for hearing our prayers. Even when we pray for the improbable, may we receive your answers in faith.

DECEMBER 2: TO BEAR WITNESS

TODAY'S PASSAGE: JOHN 1:6–8, 15, AND 19–28

Focus verse: *He himself was not the light; he came only as a witness to the light.* (John 1:8)

J ust as the apostle John's biography of Jesus opens with a poetic introduction to Jesus, the writer also gives a lyrical nod to another John, John the Baptist.

John the Baptist, as one sent by God, arrives to prepare the way to Jesus. Just as the Old Testament foretold, John comes to bear witness to the light of Jesus, to testify that he is the light of the world, the one the prophets wrote about.

The apostle John makes it clear that John the

Baptist is not the light. Instead, he is merely a witness to point people toward that light.

It's a paradox. John the Baptist will later say that Jesus will come after him, while at the same time Jesus precedes him. This certainly confused his audience back then, but it's a delightful pair of truths that we can embrace today as fact. In a physical sense, John does precede Jesus. But stepping back to view this from a heavenly perspective, we can see Jesus existing far before John was born.

The people, aware of the prophecies of the coming Savior, will see John and mistake him for the promised Messiah. But John is not the one. He is not the reincarnation of Elijah (Malachi 4:5–6 and Matthew 17:11–13). Nor is he the promised prophet (see Deuteronomy 18:15).

John will be the one who lives in the desert and preaches to the people. There he will urge them to head straight to Jesus, taking no detours and giving in to no distraction.

John will baptize people with water as a symbolic gesture, showing their sorrow (repentance) over their shortcomings (sins). In contrast, Jesus will baptize people with the Holy Spirit and fire (Matthew 3:11).

John, the greatest man ever born (Luke 7:28),

won't be worthy to unlace Jesus's sandals. As John will point to Jesus, John's importance in God's plan will decrease and Jesus's prominence will increase (John 3:30).

Questions: *Would anyone ever mistake us for Jesus? Are we building something for ourselves or pointing people to our Savior?*

Prayer: Jesus, we confess those times when we haven't put you first in our lives, haven't pointed others to you, and have wrongly accepted the praise of people, when it rightly belongs to you. Thank you for hearing our words and offering us forgiveness.

DECEMBER 3: JESUS'S FAMILY TREE
TODAY'S PASSAGE: MATTHEW 1:1–17

Focus verse: *This is the genealogy of Jesus the Messiah the son of David, the son of Abraham.* (Matthew 1:1)

W e've already talked about how John, Mark, and Luke open their biographies of Jesus. Now we'll look at Matthew's approach. Though it may seem strange to us today, Matthew begins with a tedious list of Jesus's ancestors. It's important to Matthew, as well as to his Jewish audience, that we know Jesus's ancestry—his pedigree. Especially significant is that we know Jesus is a descendant of David, as well as of Abraham. Both men received promises from God about their offspring, specifically Jesus.

This list of Jesus's genealogy includes many names we aren't familiar with and others that appear nowhere else in Scripture. Yet a few people stand out. Scanning the list, let's remember what these people did and how they connect with Jesus.

We begin with some familiar names. There's Abraham and (implicitly) his wife Sarah. Next is their son Isaac and grandson Jacob. Jacob has twelve boys; one of them is Judah. There's the sordid story of Judah and his daughter-in-law Tamar, which produces Perez.

Jumping down a few verses we see Salmon, whose name means nothing to us. Yet he marries Rahab, the former prostitute who was instrumental in God's people conquering Jericho. They have Boaz, who marries the Moabite widow, Ruth. Ruth and Boaz are the great-grandparents of David, who will become Israel's second king and is a man after God's own heart.

David and Bathsheba have Solomon. Interestingly, Bathsheba isn't mentioned by name, yet her first husband, Uriah, is. Recall that after David has his adulterous affair with Bathsheba, his attempted cover-up results in Uriah's death. Though Uriah is not a biological ancestor of Jesus,

Matthew honors Uriah by listing him in Jesus's family tree.

Next is Rehoboam. His arrogant rule results in the nation of Israel being split in two, with Rehoboam—David's royal line—ruling over the tribe of Judah. What follows is a list of kings. A few follow God, but most don't.

Of this list, we know the most about Hezekiah, a king who does much good for God but whose pride results in punishment. We may not, however, be familiar with Hezekiah's father, Ahaz. As we'll read in a couple of days, a trivial story about Ahaz results in a key prophecy about Jesus.

A few generations later, the nation of Judah is exiled into Babylon. (The nation of Israel had already been conquered by the Assyrians.) The rest of the names that follow are unfamiliar. Though they are descendants of King David, they don't serve as kings since there is no nation to rule. We know nothing else about these men through Scripture.

As we continue to scan the list of unfamiliar names, eventually we come across Joseph, the husband of Mary, who is the mother of Jesus, the Messiah.

The key point of this list is to confirm that Jesus

is a descendant of Abraham, with some of God's promises to Abraham, as well as to David, being fulfilled through Jesus.

We also see that many of Jesus's ancestors are flawed people who make serious mistakes. God blesses them anyway and uses each one, in their own time, to bring about Jesus's birth—and ultimately our salvation.

Questions: *Which of these people in Jesus's family tree do you most identify with? Whose inclusion on this list seems surprising or even shocking?*

Prayer: Lord God, thank you for your amazing plan to send Jesus to earth. Lord Jesus, thank you for dying in our place and saving us.

[Learn more about these men and women in *Old Testament Sinners and Saints: Discover What These 100 Intriguing Bible Characters Can Teach Us Today*.]

DECEMBER 4: HIGHLY FAVORED

TODAY'S PASSAGE: LUKE 1:26–30

Focus verse: *"Greetings, you who are highly favored!"*
(Luke 1:28)

Back to Luke's narrative, our story switches from foretelling the birth of John the Baptist to foretelling the birth of Jesus. Just as the angel Gabriel gave exciting news to Zechariah and Elizabeth, the angel reappears to give Mary some surprising news too.

In addition to his two appearances in the book of Luke, Gabriel also shows up in the Old Testament. He comes twice to Daniel in spiritual visions. Daniel, incidentally, also receives divine insight about the coming Savior, which we'll cover in our reading for December 6.

There's another similarity, however, between Mary and Daniel. When Gabriel comes to Mary, he calls her highly favored, for she has found favor with God. Centuries earlier, Gabriel came to Daniel and told him he was highly esteemed. To make sure Daniel didn't miss this proclamation, the angel repeated this description of Daniel being highly esteemed three times.

Mary surely knows about Daniel: his faith, godly commitment, and accomplishments, as well as his grand visions of the future. For her to view him as highly esteemed makes sense. Yet for Mary, a young teenager, being greeted by an angel proclaiming God's favor to her would be a shocking revelation. At this stage in her life, she's done nothing worthy of receiving God's favor. But isn't that what's wonderful about God's grace? We can't earn it, and we don't deserve it.

In addition to being highly favored, Gabriel also confirms that God is with her. Imagine that. Mary has God's favor, and he is with her. This goes beyond anything she may have ever hoped for or expected to occur in her life.

Gabriel's words, of course, surprise Mary. Luke

writes that she was deeply perplexed at what the angel had told her and how he had greeted her.

He then says, "Don't be afraid."

Gabriel said the same thing to Zechariah. In both cases we can imagine that Mary and Zechariah were frightened at the unexpected appearance of an angel, a supernatural being, coming to deliver God's words to them. But I'm not sure how much Gabriel's assurance to not be afraid would have calmed Mary (or Zechariah).

Then, to make sure she doesn't miss it, Gabriel tells her a second time that she has God's favor.

She is about to receive some amazing news. Though we know what this prophecy will be, Mary doesn't. Not yet.

Questions: *How does God view us? Might he see us as highly favored or highly esteemed? If an angel visited us, would we be afraid like Mary (and Zechariah)?*

Prayer: Heavenly Father, may we see ourselves as you see us. Open our eyes and our ears to receive what you tell us, even if it's perplexing or unexpected. May we not be afraid at your revelation.

DECEMBER 5: A KINGDOM THAT NEVER ENDS

TODAY'S PASSAGE: LUKE 1:31–33

Focus verse: *"He will be great and will be called the Son of the Most High."* (Luke 1:32)

Having called Mary "highly favored" and affirming that God is with her, Gabriel shocks the young girl even further. The next words out of his mouth are that she will become pregnant and have a son. She is to call him Jesus.

Though Mary is engaged to Joseph, they aren't yet married, and they won't consummate their relationship until they are. She is a virgin. With her commitment to remain pure until marriage, getting pregnant is unimaginable. So the angel's foretelling of her upcoming pregnancy is most perplexing.

Before she can voice her confusion, Gabriel continues. He tells her what her son will grow up to do.

First, Jesus will be great. Almost every version of the Bible uses this word. A few versions expand upon it, saying that Jesus will be "very great" (TLB), "the greatest among men" (VOICE), and "great *and* eminent" (AMP). "Eminent" means respected and well known. Jesus is certainly all these things—and much more.

Second, Jesus will be known as the Son of God, that is, the Son of the one who is Most High. Though Adam is the son of God (with a lowercase s; Luke 3:38), Jesus is *the* Son of God (with an uppercase s). Yes, Jesus will be Mary's son *and* he'll be God's Son, too, due to a supernatural conception through Holy Spirit power.

Third, God will give Jesus David's throne. David had a lengthy line of descendants who sat on his throne after him. Yet this continuous rule ended several centuries earlier due to the people's repeated disobedience to God. Now God will restore David's throne and give it to Jesus. This coronation won't be in a literal sense, as many of the people in Jesus's day assumed, but in the spiritual sense.

Fourth, Jesus will rule over the descendants of Jacob forever. God promised David that, through Solomon, his throne would last forever (2 Samuel 7:13). From a historical perspective, it didn't: the rule of David's descendants ended when the nation of Judah was conquered and the people were deported to Babylon. Jesus's coming to earth reestablishes a ruler over God's people.

Lastly, Jesus will have a kingdom without end, extending his reign forever into eternity. All of us who follow Jesus will live there with him (John 14:2–3).

Questions: *How can we use this prophecy about Jesus to understand him better and enhance our worship of him? Which of these five revelations might have been the hardest for Mary to comprehend? What about for us?*

Prayer: Jesus, may we understand you more fully and worship you more completely. We revere you in awe of who you are, what you have done, and what you are doing for us.

DECEMBER 6: ETERNAL KINGDOM PROPHECY

TODAY'S PASSAGE: DANIEL 7:13–14

Focus verse: *"His dominion is an everlasting dominion that will not pass away, and his kingdom is one that will never be destroyed."* (Daniel 7:14)

The prophet Daniel lived some five centuries before Mary. You may know the story of Daniel in the lions' den, where God protected him overnight after his detractors had him thrown into a den of hungry lions. The next day, the unscathed Daniel is freed and the hungry lions feast on his enemies when they're tossed in to take Daniel's place.

But the book of Daniel has much more than the

story of his escape from a den of ravenous lions. The first six chapters share six stories, including the one about the lions. The last six chapters include four future-focused prophecies that God reveals to him through visions. (The angel Gabriel, who visited Zechariah and Mary, shows up in Daniel's second and third visions.)

We read the first of his four visions in Daniel 7. In this vision he sees four winds and four great beasts. The fourth beast has ten horns. An eleventh horn appears; it has eyes and a boastful mouth.

Then Daniel sees God (the Ancient of Days) sitting on his fiery throne with a river of fire flowing before him. Millions attend him and one hundred million stand in his presence. Court is in session and the books are opened.

This is all quite perplexing, but don't stop reading. Next comes the important part, the one that anticipates Jesus.

Daniel witnesses one like a son of man, who arrives with heavenly clouds. The man approaches God and comes into his presence. He receives authority, glory, and sovereign power. People from all nations and every language worship him. His dominion will last forever, continuing without end. His kingdom will stand strong eternally.

This dream perplexes Daniel, just as it does us. He seeks an interpretation and receives one that explains the four beasts and the ten horns. When the person explaining the vision to Daniel gets to the last part, he simply says that this kingdom will last forever, and all rulers will worship and obey him (Daniel 7:27).

This final part of Daniel's vision is what Gabriel alludes to when he comes to Mary and tells her about what Jesus will do (Luke 1:32–33). Though the precise meaning of Daniel's vision may not have been clear to him then, it is clear to Gabriel when he comes to tell Mary about Jesus.

If we follow Jesus as his disciple, we're part of this everlasting kingdom that Daniel saw in his vision.

Questions: *When we read things in the Bible that don't make sense, do we seek someone (or the Holy Spirit) to explain it to us? What is our response when we see Old Testament prophecy fulfilled in the New Testament?*

Prayer: Lord God, speak to us and reveal your truth as we read the Bible. May your Word cause us to revere who you are, what you did, and your plan for us.

DECEMBER 7: HOW CAN THIS BE?

TODAY'S PASSAGE: LUKE 1:34–37

Focus verse: *"How will this be,"* Mary asked the angel, *"since I am a virgin?"* (Luke 1:34)

L et's recap. The angel Gabriel has just told Mary that she'll have a son and she's to name him Jesus. Gabriel continues his revelation to Mary, saying that Jesus will be great, the Son of God who will sit on David's throne ruling the descendants of Jacob forever in a kingdom without end.

That's a lot for Mary to take in. That would be a lot for anyone to understand.

Mary has a single question. "How?"

But she isn't asking how Jesus will be great, will

be the Son of God, or will reestablish David's throne and rule over God's people forever.

Instead, her question is about the first thing Gabriel said. It's about her giving birth to a son. How could this happen, Mary asks, "because I'm a virgin?"

How indeed.

I wonder if Mary so wondered about the "how" part as soon as Gabriel said she would get pregnant that she missed everything he said afterward, everything about who Jesus would be and what he would do.

Yet her question is also a practical one.

She knows what it takes to conceive, and she knows that she hasn't taken that step—and won't until she and Joseph complete their engagement and get married.

Whereas Gabriel didn't appreciate Zechariah's disbelief about Elizabeth's improbable pregnancy, Gabriel is patient with Mary's question. We can only speculate why.

Gabriel explains that the Holy Spirit will come upon her, and the power of God will overshadow her to supernaturally impregnate her, conceiving the holy one, the Son of God.

Frankly, I doubt this explanation clarifies

anything for the confused teenager. Her getting pregnant at this point in her life still seems incredible.

To show her that with God all things are possible, Gabriel lets Mary know that her barren relative Elizabeth is in her sixth month of pregnancy, despite her advanced years.

If God can perform a miracle in Elizabeth's womb, he can do it just as well in Mary's.

With God, all things are possible.

Questions: *Do we believe that God performs supernatural wonders today? How do we see the Holy Spirit at work in our own lives?*

Prayer: Thank you, Holy Spirit, for your miraculous work to bring Jesus to us as our Savior.

DECEMBER 8: THE VIRGIN BIRTH FORETOLD

TODAY'S PASSAGE: ISAIAH 7:1–14

Focus verse: *"The virgin will conceive and give birth to a son, and will call him Immanuel."* (Isaiah 7:14)

The prophet Isaiah lived about 150 years before Daniel and nearly seven centuries before Mary.

We've covered Daniel's prophecy stating that Jesus's kingdom will be an everlasting one. The prophet Isaiah also has prophecies about Jesus, a lot of them. The clearest, most obvious one is of his miraculous birth from a virgin. Let's look at the story surrounding this amazing prophecy.

Ahaz is king of Judah. He's a descendant of King David, some nine generations after the great king. Ahaz is also an ancestor of Jesus, preceding him by seventeen generations (see Matthew 1:6–16).

Ahaz is opposed by enemy kings, intent on capturing him and dividing the nation of Judah between them. This threat terrifies King Ahaz and the people.

God sends Isaiah to the king, telling him to take care, remain calm, and not be afraid. Isaiah confirms to Ahaz that what the enemy threatened will not occur. Judah will be spared. All Ahaz needs to do is stand firm in faith.

Then God gives Ahaz a curious command. He says, "Ask me for a sign to confirm that this is true."

"I will not," Ahaz responds. "I won't put God to the test."

This sounds like a confident, God-honoring response. Ahaz may be recalling Scripture, where God says to not test him (Deuteronomy 6:16). And later Jesus will make the same proclamation, citing this same Old Testament passage, when Satan tempts him (Matthew 4:7).

Yet God isn't pleased with Ahaz's response.

"Therefore," Isaiah says, "the Lord will give you a sign."

What is the sign?

That a "virgin will conceive and give birth to a son," who will be called Immanuel.

This improbable sign is for Ahaz to prove that God will save him from his enemies, but the deeper meaning is that it's a sign that Jesus will come to save everyone from their sins. His virgin birth will confirm it.

Mary surely knows about Isaiah's perplexing claim that a virgin would have a son. I wonder how soon she connects this prophecy with her own situation, as revealed by Gabriel. This may be why Mary so quickly accepts the angel's statement that she will have a baby boy, even though she's a virgin.

From a human standpoint, a virgin conceiving and giving birth is impossible. Yet our all-powerful (omnipotent) God can do anything.

Questions: *Does Jesus's virgin birth fill us with awe? When have we doubted God's omnipotent power to do what he says?*

Prayer: Thank you, Father God, for sending us Jesus in this unique way. May we see his virgin birth as confirmation of your plan to save us.

DECEMBER 9: GOD WITH US
TODAY'S PASSAGE: MATTHEW 1:22–23

Focus verse: *"The virgin will conceive and give birth to a son, and they will call him Immanuel" (which means "God with us").* (Matthew 1:23)

I n Luke we read about the angel Gabriel coming to Mary and telling her that as a virgin she will give birth to a son (Luke 1:30–34). Isaiah had prophetically foretold this event seven centuries earlier (Isaiah 7:14).

In Matthew's account, an angel comes to Joseph in a dream and quotes Isaiah's prophecy of a virgin birth. The child will be called Immanuel. Then the angel clarifies that Immanuel means "God with us."

God with us.

Contemplate this and don't rush past it.

God comes to earth as Jesus to be with us. He is more than a great man, a wise teacher, and the Messiah whose mission is to heal and to save. He comes to earth in physical form, as God living among us.

This is the most tangible example of God with us, but it's not the only one.

Think back to the beginning of the Bible, to creation. God, the Creator, walks with Adam and Eve, the created, in the cool of the day. He is God with them. Had they not sinned and been expelled from the garden of Eden, we could have still been there today and experienced God walking with us in the same way.

Now jump to the end of the Bible. God prepares a new heaven and a new earth. We will live with him there forever, and he will dwell with us (Revelation 21:1–3).

In the beginning, it was God walking with us. And at the end of time, it will be God dwelling with us.

Between these bookends of Scripture, where God shows his desire to be with us, we have Jesus. He comes to earth in the form of a man to be Immanuel, that is, to be God with us.

The four Gospel accounts in the Bible reveal what Jesus does on earth as God living with us. We can read his teachings and learn from his example. We can follow him as his disciple. And most importantly, we can receive his salvation that restores us into right relationship with the Father. Then we can live with him for eternity.

Yet Jesus didn't remain with us on earth in human form. He returned to heaven.

He didn't, however, leave us alone. He asked his Father to send us an advocate, the Holy Spirit, to be with us. As followers of Jesus, God's Spirit lives within us. This means that wherever we go and whatever we do, we take God with us.

Questions: *Have we thanked Jesus for coming to earth to be with us? Do we experience the Holy Spirit's presence in us today?*

Prayer: Thank you for being our God, who wants to spend time with us. Thank you for sending us the Holy Spirit to reveal truth to us and walk with us throughout our time here on earth.

DECEMBER 10: HUMBLE ACCEPTANCE

TODAY'S PASSAGE: LUKE 1:38

Focus verse: *"I am the Lord's servant,"* Mary answered. *"May your word to me be fulfilled."* (Luke 1:38)

The angel Gabriel has just delivered shocking news to Mary. It's a lot for her to take in. It would be a lot for anyone. The Holy Spirit will come upon her, and she'll get pregnant. She'll give birth to a baby boy, and he'll be the Son of God.

This is far different than what she expected her life to look like. Engaged to Joseph, they'd marry, and she hoped they'd have children. That's it.

But God has a different plan.

How will she respond? How would we respond if we were in a similar situation?

The Old Testament is filled with people who opposed God's call in their life.

Consider Gideon. The Lord's angel comes to him and calls him a mighty warrior. Gideon has questions, but the angel just tells Gideon to go out and rescue the people from the Midianites.

"How?" Gideon responds. "My family is small, and I am the least of them" (Judges 6:15). Then Gideon asks God to give him a sign. God does. Gideon asks for a second sign. God provides that too (Judges 6:38–40).

What about Jeremiah? When God calls him, he has excuses too. He says he's slow to speak, and he's too young (Jeremiah 1:6–7).

Then there's Jonah. When God tells him to go to Nineveh, Jonah disobeys. He heads in the opposite direction and sets sail for a distant city, one far away from Nineveh (Jonah 1:3).

In addition to Gideon, Jeremiah, and Jonah, there's Moses. He has many excuses about why he shouldn't do what God tells him to do. First he says, "Who am I to do such a thing?" (Exodus 3:11). Then he asks, "What if they don't believe me?" (Exodus 4:1). Then he complains that he's not a good speaker (Exodus 4:10), so God sends Aaron to help Moses and go with him.

Given the examples of these four men—each appearing prominently in the Old Testament—Mary might think she has every reason to oppose Gabriel's message.

But she doesn't.

As soon as she understands that her pregnancy will result from divine intervention, she receives Gabriel's pronouncement with humility, as God's willing servant. She accepts his plan for her life.

"May your words be fulfilled in me," Mary says.

And may God's plans for *our* lives be fulfilled in us.

Questions: *How do we react when God's plans for our life are different—perhaps far different—than our own? What might we learn from Mary's response that could better inform our own reaction to God's will for us?*

Prayer: Lord, may we receive your words to us in faith. May we accept your plan for our life as your humble, faithful servant.

DECEMBER 11: THE HOLY SPIRIT AT WORK

TODAY'S PASSAGE: LUKE 1:39–45

Focus verse: *"Blessed is she who has believed that the Lord would fulfill his promises to her!"* (Luke 1:45)

Not only will Mary have a baby, but her much older relative Elizabeth will have one too. Mary sets off to visit Elizabeth. This might be to celebrate Elizabeth's good fortune or to help prepare for the baby's arrival. Perhaps seeing Elizabeth and confirming that she is indeed pregnant, as Gabriel said, may help Mary to believe more fully the angel's pronouncement in her own life.

Regardless, Mary hurries to where Elizabeth and Zechariah live.

She arrives, enters their home, and greets Elizabeth.

At the sound of Mary's voice, Elizabeth's unborn child leaps for joy in her womb. At six months into her pregnancy, Elizabeth is at a point where she can feel baby John move inside her. And someone watching her belly may be able to see evidence of that movement as well.

Yet for the baby to *leap* inside her is both unexpected and startling. This is not a baby's normal shifting inside the womb; it's something far different. It should get our attention, just as it gets Elizabeth's.

John reacts to Mary's presence. He jumps for joy. The Holy Spirit is at work in him even before his birth. And the Holy Spirit also fills Elizabeth.

Without having modern-day communication options available to Mary, she wouldn't have had any way to let Elizabeth know she was coming to visit or about Gabriel's message to her. This means that Elizabeth would have no personal knowledge of Mary's pregnancy.

Yet through the Holy Spirit, she does. And she boldly proclaims her supernatural insight. She calls Mary blessed and she blesses the child Mary will bear. She says this with a confident loudness.

Elizabeth knows who this child is. In what would be an otherwise-cryptic rhetorical question, she asks, "Who am I that the mother of *my* Lord should come to visit me?" By calling Mary "the mother of my Lord," she recognizes the divine nature of Mary's baby. Elizabeth realizes that he is God—and her Lord.

Then she blesses Mary for believing what God had told her.

Elizabeth says all these things based completely on Holy Spirit insight.

Questions: *How good are we at hearing the Holy Spirit and reacting to what he says? What can we do today to bless or encourage someone?*

Prayer: Holy Spirit, speak to us and reveal your truth. May we hear your voice and respond with confidence.

DECEMBER 12: MARY'S HUMBLE WORSHIP

TODAY'S PASSAGE: LUKE 1:46–48

Focus verse: *"My soul glorifies the Lord and my spirit rejoices in God my Savior."* (Luke 1:46–47)

Through Holy Spirit insight, Elizabeth has just blessed Mary for the child that she will bear and for believing what God had promised. Mary responds with a song. It's her psalm of praise, which includes a bit of prophecy too.

Mary physically sings (through her *body*) that her *soul* glorifies God, and her *spirit* rejoices in him as her Savior. Body, soul, and spirit.

Paul will later write about these three parts of our being: spirit, soul, and body (1 Thessalonians 5:23). Some modern-day teachers build upon this verse, explaining that we are a spirit, we have a soul (our mind, will, and emotions), and we live in the body. Together these three aspects make up our being. Mary praises God through all three. How this must please the Almighty.

May we worship God just like Mary.

She praises him because he's aware of her humble state as his willing servant.

The Bible talks much about humility. Jesus, her son, will later say that those who lift themselves up will be humbled, but the humble will be exalted (Luke 14:11). Jesus's brother James, another son of Mary, will later encourage people to humble themselves before God so that he can lift them up (James 4:10). James also says that God opposes the proud and favors the humble (James 4:6, which paraphrases Proverbs 3:34).

Jesus's disciple Peter will also address humility. He tells his audience to be compassionate and humble (1 Peter 3:8). Beyond that, he later encourages the people to cover themselves with humility. Then God will lift them up (1 Peter 5:5–6, which also paraphrases Proverbs 3:34).

A recurring theme in these verses is that God will exalt the humble, that he'll lift them up. And God will exalt Mary, as his humble servant, more than any other. In her humble state as God's servant, Mary makes a prophetic declaration that seems anything but humble.

Since it's a prophecy, it comes from the Holy Spirit. Through his supernatural insight, Mary proclaims that all generations will call her blessed. And, indeed, we have done just that.

We bless the Virgin Mary who humbly served as God's vessel to bring Jesus into our world to heal and save us.

Questions: *How can we better praise God through our body, soul, and spirit? What can we learn from Mary's humility to apply to our lives today?*

Prayer: Heavenly Father, thank you for your promise that you will exalt the humble. Instead of trying to lift ourselves up, may we patiently wait for you to do so at the right time.

DECEMBER 13: PRAISING GOD THROUGH SCRIPTURE

TODAY'S PASSAGE: LUKE 1:49–55

Focus verse: *"Holy is his name."* (Luke 1:49)

Mary continues her psalm of praise by commending God for who he is. Her recitation of his attributes builds on Old Testament truths, quotes, and allusions, presenting an informed scriptural understanding of how God has been at work.

She starts by declaring that he has done great things, which is supported by Psalm 71:19. And his name is holy (Psalm 111:9). Also, consider Isaiah's vision where he sees seraphim praising God as "Holy, holy, holy" (Isaiah 6:3).

Next, she affirms that God offers mercy to those

who fear him generation after generation. This comes from God, through Moses, in what we call the Ten Commandments (Exodus 20:5–6).

Mary continues praising God for the mighty deeds he has performed (Psalm 98:1) through the strength of his arm (Isaiah 40:10). In doing so he scatters the proud (Genesis 11:8).

God removes kings from their thrones (Daniel 4:31) and lifts the humble (2 Samuel 22:28, Psalm 18:27, and Psalm 147:6).

God also feeds the hungry and gives them what is good (Psalm 107:9).

In addition, God helps his servant Israel (that is, God's chosen people) and shows them his mercy by providing salvation (Psalm 89:3) to Abraham and his descendants forever, just as he promised (Exodus 32:13 and Deuteronomy 7:8).

This passage in Luke shows Mary's deep knowledge of Scripture and her ability to weave disparate passages effectively into her psalm of praise. She has surely hidden his word in her heart (Psalm 119:11).

Though Mary's song looks back to what God has done, it's also a hopeful confidence in what he will do through Jesus, the child that she will soon bear. It looks forward to the salvation he will offer to all future generations.

As such, Mary's prayer emerges as a timeless testimony to the Almighty Lord.

Questions: *How well do we know God's Holy Word? How can we give it back to him as a song of praise in reverent worship, just like Mary did?*

Prayer: Father God, may we read, learn, and meditate on your Word. Holy Spirit, speak to us and give us greater understanding of what the Bible says. Jesus, thank you for coming to save us from our sins.

[Mary's Song in Luke 1:46–55 is also called the Song of Mary, the Canticle of Mary, or the Magnificat (Mary's Magnificat), as in "My soul magnifies the Lord." This song of praise reads like a psalm. Learn more about other psalms scattered throughout Scripture in the book *Beyond Psalm 150: Discover More Sacred Songs of Praise, Petition, and Lament throughout the Bible*.]

DECEMBER 14: JOHN'S BIRTH
TODAY'S PASSAGE: LUKE 1:56–66

Focus verse: *Everyone who heard this wondered about it, asking, "What then is this child going to be?"* (Luke 1:66)

Remember that when the angel Gabriel appeared before Mary, he told her that Elizabeth was six months pregnant. Mary hurried to visit her relative and stayed for three months. Though the Bible doesn't specify it, it's safe to assume that Mary stays until John's birth and then returns home.

Just as Gabriel had told Zechariah, Elizabeth gives birth to a son. Recall that Elizabeth is quite old at this point, so having a baby at her age is most unlikely. When her friends and family hear about this incredible news, they celebrate with her for God's amazing mercy for giving her a child at last.

After eight days, it's time to circumcise and name the baby. Everyone assumes his parents will call him Zechariah, after his father. But Elizabeth insists he's not to be named after his dad. Instead, his name will be John, even though they have no one in their family with that name.

The people question this and want confirmation. They make signs to Zechariah to find out what he wants the child's name to be. This is because Zechariah was unable to speak—and, it seems, unable to hear—after he questioned Gabriel's improbable news that Elizabeth would become pregnant in her old age, even though they'd been praying for that precise thing for years.

Zechariah signals for a writing tablet and indicates, "His name is John."

As soon as he confirms the baby's name, he regains his ability to speak. With his first words, he praises God.

The people are amazed and overwhelmed with awe. The news spreads quickly, and everyone in the area begins talking about these events: the elderly Elizabeth having a son, his parents giving him an unexpected name contrary to convention, and the mute Zechariah miraculously having his speech restored.

God has their attention, and the people wonder about John and what he's going to grow up to do.

Though it seems impossible, God has just given an old woman a child. This prepares the way for another miracle: A virgin will give birth.

Questions: *Do we really believe that with God all things are possible? Do we have the faith to pray for and expect to receive the improbable?*

Prayer: Father God, may we be in awe of who you are, what you have done, and what you will do. May we walk in faith and receive your gifts with a thankful heart.

DECEMBER 15: ZECHARIAH'S HOLY SPIRIT PROPHECY

TODAY'S PASSAGE: LUKE 1:67–80

Focus verse: *"And you, my child, will be called a prophet of the Most High."* (Luke 1:76)

As soon as Zechariah confirms that his son is to be named John, he regains his ability to talk. The first thing he does is praise God. Luke records Zechariah's song of praise, which offers a Holy Spirit-inspired prophecy.

We may assume Zechariah's words look forward to what John will do when he grows up, but Zechariah actually begins by talking about Jesus (Luke 1:68–75). We know this because he refers to a child from the house of David, who comes from the tribe of Judah. Jesus comes from the tribe of Judah, a descendant of David. John does not. Zechariah and Elizabeth are both descendants of Aaron, from the tribe of Levi. Clearly Zechariah isn't talking about his son, but Mary's son Jesus, who is also the Son of God.

Consider Jesus as we study these verses. Even though Jesus won't be born for another six months, Zechariah—under Holy Spirit influence—speaks as though his birth has already occurred.

Zechariah praises God because—through Jesus —he has come to redeem them, providing them with a strong king—a descendant of David—to save them, just as the prophets foretold (Jeremiah 23:5–6).

This new king will provide salvation for them from their enemies, the people who hate them. He'll make a way for them to serve God, in holy righteousness, without fear, for the rest of their life.

Zechariah's words echo the assumption of many people in his day, that the coming Savior will rescue them from the tyranny of an oppressor nation. Yet this isn't why Jesus comes. He comes to save the people from the grip of the oppression of sin.

This is what God promised to the people's

ancestors through his covenant made with Abraham. And this is what Jesus will fulfill when he dies on the cross for our sins and rises from the dead to save us.

Having praised God and prophesied about Jesus, Zechariah shifts his attention to prophesying about what his son John will do. He'll be a prophet of the Most High God and prepare the way for Jesus, teaching the people about salvation, which will come through the forgiveness of our sins.

Jesus will shine like the sun, coming from heaven, to reveal what hides in the dark. The apostle John will later write that Jesus is a shining light, overcoming darkness (John 1:4–5).

Zechariah's son, John the Baptist, is not the expected Savior, but he will precede him (John 3:28).

Questions: *Are we open to receive Holy Spirit inspiration and tell others what he reveals to us? How can we point others to Jesus?*

Prayer: Holy Spirit, may you direct our praise to

God and reveal truth to us. And when you do, may we receive, accept, and believe what you tell us.

[This is another passage that reads like a psalm. To explore other psalms scattered throughout Scripture, see *Beyond Psalm 150: Discover More Sacred Songs of Praise, Petition, and Lament throughout the Bible*.]

DECEMBER 16: LAW-ABIDING AND RIGHTEOUS JOSEPH

TODAY'S PASSAGE: MATTHEW 1:18–19

Focus verse: *Joseph her husband was faithful to the law.*
(Matthew 1:19)

The revelation of Mary's pregnancy is recorded in the book of Luke. Now let's consider the situation from Joseph's perspective, which comes from the book of Matthew.

Mary is engaged to Joseph, pledged to become his wife. But before they consummate their relationship, she gets pregnant. We don't know if she tells Joseph the astonishing news as soon as Gabriel reveals it to her or if she waits and tells Joseph later. Perhaps it's only after the physical changes in her body become clear to all that she admits to Joseph what is happening and why.

Her claim that she's pregnant through the Holy Spirit, however, would come across to Joseph as a preposterous explanation. Who would believe that? No one. This isn't how conception happens—at least it never has happened this way before (or since).

How disappointed Joseph must be. The pure young girl that he's marrying isn't so chaste after all. How could Joseph have been so wrong about her character? He trusted her to wait, yet she was unfaithful. To add to her deceit, she gives an outrageous story to explain her seeming infidelity.

Getting pregnant before marriage will be a stigma she'll carry with her the rest of her life. According to their tradition, Mary could be killed for getting pregnant outside of marriage (see Genesis 38:24 and Deuteronomy 22:22).

Additionally, people will assume that Joseph— her betrothed—is the father of her child. This will be something that he, too, will carry with him the rest of his life. To protect his reputation, the wise solution would be to publicly proclaim that he's not the father and permanently end his relationship with her.

Yet Joseph doesn't want to openly pronounce his disappointment and expose her dishonor. He seeks to break off their engagement quietly and not cause Mary any more disgrace.

In this way he can still be faithful to the law of God, while also offering her undeserved kindness. Doing so also hints that he still cares for Mary, despite what he believes she did.

Questions: *If we were Joseph, how would we have responded when we found out our fiancée was pregnant? Are we willing to put the welfare of others above our reputation?*

Prayer: Lord God, may Joseph's righteous character inspire us and inform our attitudes and actions.

DECEMBER 17: OBEDIENT JOSEPH
TODAY'S PASSAGE: MATTHEW 1:20–25

Focus verse: *When Joseph woke up, he did what the angel of the Lord had commanded him and took Mary home as his wife.* (Matthew 1:24)

Learning of Mary's unexpected pregnancy, Joseph intends to privately end their engagement. As he mulls over the best way to do this, he has a dream. As he sleeps, an angel comes to him with a message from God.

First, the angel addresses him as Joseph, son of David. It's easy to rush by this label, but just a few verses before this passage, Matthew names Joseph's father as Jacob. The angel's reference to the son of David alludes to King David, a distant ancestor of

Joseph. Calling him the son of David reminds Joseph of the promises God made to that king. One pledge is that his descendants would rule forever in a kingdom that will never end (2 Samuel 7:16). Joseph is part of this royal line, as will be his offspring, including Jesus as his stepson.

Next, the angel tells Joseph to not worry about taking Mary as his wife. The life inside her was indeed conceived by the Holy Spirit, a spiritual act and not a physical one through Mary's infidelity. Though Mary has already told him these facts—as unbelievable as they seemed—hearing the angel's confirmation corroborates her story. How relieved this must make Joseph, knowing that she did no wrong and her virtue is still intact.

The angel then says she will give birth to a son, and they are to name him Jesus. These are the same two pieces of information that the angel Gabriel had already given to Mary, further confirming the accuracy of what Mary had told her fiancé.

Jesus, the angel tells Joseph, will save the people from their sins. In contrast, Gabriel had told Mary that Jesus will reign forever in a never-ending kingdom. These two proclamations are not, however, in contradiction to each other.

To save all people, Jesus will die for their sins

and rise from the grave to show his mastery over death. Then he will assume his rule forever. Jesus's saving act provides for his eternal kingdom.

When Joseph wakes up from his dream, he does as the angel commanded. He takes Mary into his home as his wife. But to keep her virgin status intact, they remain celibate until after Jesus is born.

Questions: *How does God speak to us? When he tells us to do something, do we obey?*

Prayer: Thank you, Jesus, for coming to earth to save us and establishing your rule in a kingdom that never ends.

[We've already covered the middle of today's passage, Matthew 1:22–23, in the reading for December 9.]

DECEMBER 18: THE JOURNEY
TODAY'S PASSAGE: LUKE 2:1–5

Focus verse: *Joseph also went up from the town of Nazareth in Galilee to Judea, to Bethlehem the town of David.* (Luke 2:4)

As our journey toward Jesus's birth unfolds, another complication arises. Caesar Augustus decrees that a census will take place for the entire Roman Empire. Everyone—including Joseph, with pregnant Mary—must return to their hometown to register. They travel from where they live in Nazareth, which is in the region of Galilee, to the region of Judea, specifically to the town of Bethlehem.

God uses Caesar Augustus's census to

temporarily move Joseph and Mary. This enables Jesus to be born in Bethlehem, just as foretold in the Old Testament by the prophet Micah (Micah 5:2).

The Old Testament doesn't mention the town of Nazareth, but it does talk about Bethlehem. Bethlehem was the home of Boaz, who married the Moabite widow Ruth. They were the great-grandparents of David, who would later become king.

Luke adds a confusing note about Bethlehem, calling it the town of David (the city of David). When we think of the City of David, we think of Jerusalem, which is a few miles away. However, Luke uses *town* or *city* generically, while the Old Testament refers to the City of David (uppercase c) as a proper noun. The two are different and we shouldn't confuse them.

Given that Mary's pregnancy is nearing completion, the timing of this journey is challenging. Modern-day maps show that the route from Nazareth to Bethlehem is about 90 miles (145 km). Though we often picture Mary making this journey riding on a donkey, the Bible doesn't say that.

Traveling 90 miles would be difficult for anyone, be it on foot or on the back of an animal. For a pregnant woman about to give birth, the trip must be a most trying journey.

Regardless of the method of transportation, the trip would have taken four to five days in normal circumstances. At a typical pace of 2.5 mph (4 kph) and walking eight hours a day, they'd arrive in Bethlehem in four and a half days. Yet Mary's condition surely adds time to the trip, with frequent stops so that she can rest or relieve herself.

Questions: *Does seeing Old Testament prophecy fulfilled in the New Testament fill us with awe? Might Mary and Joseph have been thinking about this as they traveled from Nazareth to Bethlehem?*

Prayer: Lord God, we stand in amazement at how you orchestrated events so Jesus could be born in Bethlehem, just as your prophet Micah said would happen. Thank you for revealing this insight to us through your Word.

DECEMBER 19: THE WORD BECAME FLESH

TODAY'S PASSAGE: JOHN 1:14–18

Focus verse: *The Word became flesh and made his dwelling among us.* (John 1:14)

As we move closer to Jesus's birth, recall the apostle John's poetic opening to his biography of Jesus. In it, John refers to Jesus, saying that "In the beginning was the Word" (John 1:1) and that "In him was life, and that life was the light of all mankind" (John 1:4).

Later in that passage, John writes that "The Word became flesh." That is, Jesus—who helped create us at the formation of our reality—left his supernatural home in the spiritual realm to join us here on earth as a flesh-and-blood person.

What would it have been like to see Jesus and hear him? I envy his followers who walked with him, ate with him, and lived with him. What would it have been like to watch his miracles take place and witness his confrontations with religious leaders? If only we could have experienced Jesus in real life instead of merely reading about him in the Bible.

Yes, Jesus lived with us, his creation. Imagine that. The Creator dwelling with his creation. The idea, however, isn't unprecedented.

In the garden of Eden, God spent time with his creation, walking with them in the cool of the day (Genesis 3:8). This is what our Lord intended from the beginning: he would walk with us, and we with him. Yet Adam and Eve sinned and were removed from the garden, along with the privilege of spending in-person time with their Creator.

Now Jesus arrives to live among his creation, to walk with them. Yet when it comes time for Jesus to leave this earth (after his death and resurrection) he doesn't want to leave his followers alone. Instead, he asks his Father to send them another advocate, to help them and be with them forever. This advocate is the Holy Spirit (John 14:16–17). The Holy Spirit will teach them and remind them of everything he said (John 14:26).

Though Jesus will physically leave his followers, he'll remain with them supernaturally through the Holy Spirit. In this way, he'll continue to live with them—and with us. And what else is Jesus going to do? He's going to prepare a place for us for when we die (John 14:2).

Just as God walked with us at the beginning of time, he will do so at the end of time too. God will once again dwell with his people (Revelation 21:3), just as he once did in the garden of Eden. He invites us—all those who follow him—to drink the water of life (Revelation 22:17) and live with him forever in his new heaven and new earth (Revelation 21:1–3).

Jesus coming to earth as a person and living with his creation is unparalleled throughout all of time. Yet it's foreshadowed at creation and will be reinstated at the end of time. Even today Jesus lives with us through the Holy Spirit.

Questions: *What would we have done if we had lived when Jesus walked this earth? How well do we do now to respond to the Holy Spirit's presence within us as he teaches us about Jesus and reminds us of what he said?*

Prayer: Holy Spirit, reveal truth to us and teach us about Jesus. When you speak, may we have ears to hear what you say.

DECEMBER 20: FOR TO US A CHILD IS BORN

TODAY'S PASSAGE: ISAIAH 9:1–7

Focus verse: *For to us a child is born, to us a son is given.* (Isaiah 9:6)

This passage in Isaiah's prophecy opens with the word *nevertheless*. To gain insight as to what this means we must consider the end of the prior chapter. There Isaiah writes of the time when the people have turned their backs on God and are suffering the consequences of their actions. They see only distress, darkness, and gloom.

Nevertheless, there will come a future time when the gloom of those in distress will fade. The people, those walking in darkness, will see a great light. It's the dawn of a new day (see John 1:4–5). In that time there will be joy and rejoicing. But why?

Because a child will be born, God's Son sent to earth to save us. His name will be Jesus (Matthew 1:21 and Luke 1:31), and he'll be called Wonderful, Counselor, Mighty God, Everlasting Father, and Prince of Peace. What a profound list of names; what an impressive record of his attributes.

As **Wonderful**, Jesus will be admirable and elicit astonishment from all who see him.

As **Counselor**, Jesus will teach us. Matthew, Mark, Luke, and John record his words, along with his actions for us to emulate. Though we think of the Holy Spirit as our Counselor, remember that the characteristics of one part of the Trinity apply to all.

As **Mighty God**, Jesus will show everyone his almighty power. He'll heal people, raise the dead, and forgive sins.

As **Everlasting Father**, he lives eternally.

And as **Prince of Peace**, he will usher in a time of harmony.

Ruling on David's throne, this child will grow up to carry the government on his shoulders. He'll reign over his kingdom with justice and right-eousness from that time forward and forevermore.

Imagine living under a political power that provides both a just and a right leadership, governing without fault or variation.

All this arrives through Jesus and begins when he comes to earth as a child to live among us.

Part of Isaiah's prophecy is fulfilled with the Savior's birth, with Jesus's arrival establishing the framework for much of the remaining details of the prophet's declaration. We eagerly await the complete fulfillment of it when we, as his church, marry the Lamb (Revelation 19:7).

And this all begins when Father God sends his one and only Son into our world to save us (John 3:16–17).

Questions: *What kind of future do we have because of Jesus? How can we best live our life now as we await our final destination with him?*

Prayer: Jesus, may we live each day for you, mindful of who you are and what you did for us. Continue to teach us through the Holy Spirit and prepare us to live with you for eternity.

[Learn more in *Isaiah Bible Study: Discover Jesus, Justice, and Gentiles through the Prophet's Timeless Words.*]

DECEMBER 21: THE BIRTH
TODAY'S PASSAGE: LUKE 2:6–7

Focus verse: *She wrapped him in cloths and placed him in a manger.* (Luke 2:7)

After traveling for at least five days, and possibly six or seven, Joseph and Mary arrive in Bethlehem.

Micah prophesied that from Bethlehem would come one to rule over Israel. His origin is from ancient times, that is, from long ago (Micah 5:2). This mention of *origin* would have been cryptic to the people then, but it makes sense to us today, given that the ruler who is to come, Jesus, also took part in creation.

When Mary and Joseph arrive in Bethlehem, they're no doubt exhausted—especially Mary. But there's no place for them to stay. All the inns are full of other people who have already arrived for the census. No one invites them into their home, something we often see practiced in the Old Testament (Genesis 19:2, Judges 19:15–20, and Job 31:32; also see Matthew 25:35 and Hebrews 13:2).

One person, however, does have compassion on them and lets them stay in their barn along with the animals. At least Mary and Joseph have shelter.

There in the barn, amid the filth of the animals, Mary goes into labor. Surely this is not what she expected for the birth of her baby. She planned to be at home with family surrounding her—supporting her—when the time came. We can imagine that she knew the local midwife in Nazareth and had arranged for the woman's aid with her delivery.

Yet this is not how things unfold. The only family with her is Joseph, her fiancé. She has no other relatives around. If a local midwife from Bethlehem arrives to help with the delivery, it's not someone Mary knows. And if there's no midwife, it's up to Joseph to comfort Mary and deliver her child.

Regardless of the situation, Jesus is born. Mary and Joseph clean him and wrap him in cloths. Lacking a crib or other suitable place for him to sleep, they lay him in a manger, an animal feeding trough.

In this way, the long-expected Messiah enters the world, arriving in the humblest of conditions and existing in the most austere setting. Surely this is an inappropriate welcome to the King of kings and Lord of lords.

Mary, the one we now call blessed, doesn't seem so blessed at this time. God chose her for a most momentous role. Yet so far, she's had to endure getting pregnant before she was married, traveling a long distance in her ninth month of pregnancy, and giving birth to a baby in a barn in an unfamiliar town.

If I were Mary, I would have expected a bit more from God. Fortunately, as we'll soon see, Mary has a much better perspective.

Questions: *When God calls us to do something for him, do we expect everything to unfold perfectly? When surprises come up along the way, do we accept them in faith or complain?*

Prayer: Lord, we thank you for Mary, your humble and willing servant, who accepted your plan for her life. May her actions inspire us and may we follow her example.

DECEMBER 22: BREAKING NEWS

TODAY'S PASSAGE: LUKE 2:8–12

Focus verse: *"Today in the town of David a Savior has been born to you; he is the Messiah, the Lord."* (Luke 2:11)

Jesus has just been born. The long-awaited Messiah, as the prophets foresaw, has at last come to earth to save his people. This is wonderful news. The best news yet.

But who else on earth knows about it? Just Joseph and Mary. That's it. No one else is aware that salvation has finally arrived, albeit in the form of an infant.

To whom should God proclaim this breaking news?

Consider Herod. He's the area's leading political figure. People would listen to him. Tell him about Jesus, and soon everyone would know.

But not so fast. As we'll soon see, when the Magi tell Herod about the birth of a new king, he reacts with jealousy. He wants to kill the baby before the boy can do any harm to the king's rule. No, Herod is not a wise choice.

Let's then consider religious leaders. The high priest seems like a wise choice. Or how about a group of chief priests? Or send an angel to announce Jesus's arrival in front of the entire Jewish Council, the Sanhedrin.

Though this seems like the ideal group, they are not. They will later oppose Jesus's ministry and dismiss him. He represents change to their religious status quo. His teaching opposes their authority, leadership, and prestige. Ultimately, they'll react just like Herod, with jealous, murderous intent.

Who then? What about people at the temple? Or if there's a synagogue in Bethlehem, what about the synagogue leader? Or the town's mayor? The leading people? These are all astute ideas, too, but these individuals could easily respond just as the religious elite will later do in Jerusalem.

Who then would accept the announcement of Jesus's arrival as the good news it is? Who would celebrate it and not oppose it?

God dispatches his angel to carry this breaking news to an unassuming group of shepherds as they watch over their flocks in the middle of the night. Shrouded in darkness, with only the dim light of a campfire or the glow of the stars, the angel's bright arrival shocks these shepherds. They're terrified.

But the angel says, "Don't be afraid. I have great news for all people. Today, the Messiah you've been expecting has been born in Bethlehem. To confirm who he is, you'll find him wrapped up in cloths and sleeping in a manger."

Telling the lowly and unassuming shepherds about Jesus's birth is how God decides to let the people know that his promises are at last unfolding.

Questions: *If we're not in leadership or an esteemed position, do we think God can still speak to us and use us to carry out his will? And if we are in a position of authority, do we care more about how God is at work, or do we simply want to maintain the status quo and our station in life?*

Prayer: Lord, may we be receptive to what you are doing in our world and receive with gladness what you tell us.

DECEMBER 23: HEAVENLY PRAISE
TODAY'S PASSAGE: LUKE 2:13–14

Focus verse: *A great company of the heavenly host appeared with the angel, praising God.* (Luke 2:13)

The shepherds are out in the fields keeping an eye on their sheep and minding their own business. It's the middle of the night. Then an angel shows up, startles them, and gives them wonderful news. But one angel isn't enough. There are more. Many more.

A celestial throng suddenly joins the angel.

Luke describes them as a "great company" and a "heavenly host." It's an evocative description, but also a bit vague.

A *great company* suggests there are many of them,

but we don't know how many. Is it ten, a hundred, or a thousand? Even more? And does *heavenly host* mean they're angels or some other supernatural beings? (Luke later mentions angels, plural, so we can assume the heavenly host is made up, at least in part, of angels. See Luke 2:15.)

And where are they? We often envision them in the sky, hovering in place with their angel wings. But Luke simply says they appear with the angel. If the angel is standing on the ground or levitating at eye level, this must be where the heavenly host is too.

Now consider their form of communication. Are they singing? We assume so, but they may not be. They may chant or speak these words. Do they communicate in unison or harmony?

Next consider the message. Did Luke record everything they sang, chanted, or said? Do they share this message once or repeat it over and over? Is there more to their declaration, with Luke only reporting on the refrain, summary, or key part of the message?

Take a moment and let your imagination consider these questions as you envision these two verses from a fresh perspective.

Though our assumption of what took place and

the pictures we've seen about this event may be wrong, or at least misleading, this isn't the point. The point is that this large group of supernatural beings praises God. Consider what they say.

They give glory to God on his heavenly throne.

They proclaim peace to the earth, specifically those he favors. That is, glorious God gives peace to those he chooses.

This praise comes right after the angel's announcement of Jesus's birth. Therefore, the two must connect: God in his glory sends us Jesus to bring peace to those he esteems.

Glory. Peace. Favor.

Thank you, Jesus.

Questions: *Do we give God the glory he deserves? How can we praise God?*

Prayer: Thank you, Jesus, for coming to earth to reveal God's glory and usher in peace to those he favors.

DECEMBER 24: LET'S GO SEE JESUS

TODAY'S PASSAGE: TODAY'S PASSAGE: LUKE
2:15–18, 20

Focus verse: *When they had seen him, they spread the word concerning what had been told them about this child.*

(Luke 2:17)

After sharing the astounding news of Jesus's arrival with the shepherds, the angels leave. Amazed by the experience, the shepherds discuss what happened. They've never experienced anything like this before and don't know anyone else who has either.

As they consider what has just occurred, they decide they should go to Bethlehem to check out what the angels told them.

They have only two clues. The first is that the baby is in the town of David, which they know to mean Bethlehem (1 Samuel 17:12). It's nearby. The other is that the baby will be using a manger—an animal feeding trough—for a bed. This suggests that he'll be in a barn, an open-sided shed, or even outside in a corral and not in a house or inn.

We don't know how long it takes the shepherds to get to Bethlehem, only that it's nearby. We also don't know how long they must search before they find baby Jesus. But once they see a child wrapped in cloths and lying in the manger, they have no doubt who it is. It's exactly as the angel explained.

We also don't know how long they stay with Mary, Joseph, and baby Jesus. But when they leave, they tell others. And what a story they have to share: the angel's message, the heavenly host praising God, and finding the baby who will save their nation. He's the Messiah they've been expecting, the Lord.

Luke writes that the people who hear the shepherds' message are amazed. While some could embrace this good news with relief and God-honoring astonishment, others might receive it with skepticism, declaring that it's too improbable or that the shepherds aren't credible witnesses.

Regardless, the shepherds create quite a stir as they spread word of Jesus's arrival.

Then they return to their sheep, giving God glory and praise for what they've been told and have seen.

The shepherds provide us a good mode to follow when we discover something amazing about God through the Bible, the Holy Spirit, or other teachers. First, we should investigate what we've heard (see Acts 17:11). Then, once we confirm it's true, we should tell others about it; we spread the word. And we conclude by giving God glory and praise for it all.

The good news of Jesus is just as important today as it was when he arrived 2,000 years ago. May we follow the shepherds' example and spread the word.

Questions: *Who can we tell about the good news of Jesus? When have we last given God glory and praise for sending Jesus to earth to save us?*

Prayer: Heavenly Father, thank you for sending Jesus to earth as our Savior. Jesus, thank you for

dying for our mistakes—our sins—to reconcile us
with Father God.

DECEMBER 25: TREASURING AND PONDERING

TODAY'S PASSAGE: LUKE 2:19

Focus verse: *But Mary treasured up all these things and pondered them in her heart.* (Luke 2:19)

Mary's delivery had been a private experience. Now a bunch of strangers show up. They're nearby shepherds who have left their sheep unattended to make a surprise visit. Jesus might only be a few hours old at this time. What began as a private experience between Mary, Joseph, and some farm animals has turned into a public event.

The shepherds have an astonishing story to share. They talk about an angel giving them a surprising message. Having experienced this herself nine months earlier, Mary knows all about angels delivering messages from God.

But these shepherds also talk about a heavenly host praising God for the baby Mary has just birthed. This reminds her of what Gabriel had earlier told her about who Jesus would become and what he would do, confirming the angel's words and his extraordinary prophecy.

The last nine months have certainly been an incredible experience for Mary. It is indeed something to ponder and treasure. In addition to the miracle of birth, Mary's pregnancy has been surrounded by astonishing, unprecedented events.

First there was Gabriel's pronouncement that she would conceive through the Holy Spirit and give birth to the Savior that her people had been expecting for centuries, as foretold by the prophets.

Then there was Elizabeth's pregnancy in her old age, her being filled with the Holy Spirit, and having baby John leap for joy inside his mother's womb at the mere sound of Mary's voice.

Next there was Joseph receiving supernatural insight through a dream. He stuck by Mary when the religiously proper thing to do—the socially expected response—would be to sever all ties with her for a pregnancy he had nothing to do with.

Now these shepherds show up with more astounding news.

It's a lot to contemplate, and it's a lot for Mary to treasure in her heart and ponder.

Questions: *How well do we do at pondering the good news of Jesus? Do we treasure in our hearts the many things he did for us—and continues to do?*

Prayer: Help us to never forget, Lord, the awe of Jesus's amazing, supernatural arrival here on earth. May we treasure his birth in our hearts and never stop pondering what he has done for us.

DECEMBER 26: THE TWELVE DAYS OF CHRISTMAS

TODAY'S PASSAGE: PSALM 90:12–17

Focus verse: *Teach us to number our days, that we may gain a heart of wisdom.* (Psalm 90:12)

Traditionally, the Christmas season starts on Christmas Day and lasts for the next twelve days until Epiphany on January 6, which marks the arrival of the Magi.

We have moved steadily through Advent to the birth of Jesus, and we now shift to The Twelve Days of Christmas, also known as Twelvetide.

The well-known song "The Twelve Days of Christmas" is either memorable or annoying, depending on perspective. Contrary to what some think, the song wasn't intended to have any connection to Christianity.

However, it might be fun to come up with our own list for the twelve days of Christmas.

Twelve Disciples: Jesus calls twelve disciples to follow him. They are Simon (Peter), Andrew, James, John, Philip, Bartholomew, Matthew, Thomas, James son of Alphaeus, Simon the Zealot, Judas son of James, and Judas Iscariot (Luke 6:13–16). They're sometimes called "the twelve." Having twelve disciples symbolically parallels the twelve tribes of Israel.

Eleven Remaining Disciples: After Judas Iscariot betrays Jesus, he hangs himself in remorse. Now we're down to eleven, sometimes called "the eleven" (Luke 24:9). Later the eleven add Matthias to bring their number back up to twelve (Acts 1:26), but then Herod kills James (Acts 12:1–2), reducing the number back to eleven.

Ten Healed Lepers: Jesus heals ten lepers and sends them off to the priest so they can be declared clean, but only one returns to thank him (Luke 17:11–19).

Nine O'clock: Jesus is crucified at nine in the morning (Mark 15:25). Though Christmas is a time to celebrate Jesus's arrival on earth, we must remember that he came to die in our place (Good Friday) and overcome death (Easter).

Eight Days Old: On the eighth day after Jesus's birth, Mary and Joseph circumcise him (Leviticus 12:3) and name him Jesus (Luke 2:21), just as the angels instructed them (Matthew 1:21 and Luke 1:31).

Seven Demons Defeated: Jesus casts seven demons out of Mary Magdalene (Luke 8:2). This reminds us that he came to both heal *and* to save (consider Jeremiah 17:14).

Six Stone Jars: There are six stone water jars at the wedding in Cana. In Jesus's first recorded public miracle he turns the water in those containers into wine, really good wine (John 2:1–11).

Five Loaves of Bread: Jesus feeds 5,000 men (plus women and children) by miraculously multiplying five loaves of bread and two fish. Everyone eats as much as they want, and they even have leftovers (Luke 9:10–17).

Four Loyal Friends: Four men carry their paralyzed friend to Jesus on a stretcher. Jesus forgives the man of his sins. Then, to prove he has the power to forgive sins, he also heals the man (Mark 2:1–12).

Three Days Dead: Jesus is crucified and dead for three days before he rises from the grave (Mark 8:31 and John 2:18–22; also see Matthew 27:63).

Two Small Coins: A poor woman places two small copper coins in the offering. Jesus affirms her for it, saying that she put in more than all the others combined (Luke 21:1–4).

One Savior: Jesus is the one and only Son of God sent to us from the Father (John 1:14) to save us (John 3:16).

Questions: *Which of these numbers surprises you the most? Why? What significant biblical events or characters would you add to this list?*

Prayer: As we celebrate the twelve days of Christmas, may we be mindful of all Jesus did for us when he was here on earth. And may we follow him as his disciple throughout the rest of our lives.

DECEMBER 27: THE EIGHTH DAY
TODAY'S PASSAGE: LUKE 2:21–24

Focus verse: *He was named Jesus, the name the angel had given him before he was conceived.* (Luke 2:21)

The shepherds arrived shortly after Jesus's birth to see the child the angel had told them about. Our story picks up eight days later, when it's time to circumcise him.

We're left to consider what happened in the days between these two events. Is this a private time for Mary and Joseph to spend adapting to the needs of a newborn and learning to care for him? Do they spend time in awe, marveling at baby Jesus, contemplating who he will become, and considering what he will do?

I suspect they do, but they may also have some unexpected guests show up too. Remember, when the shepherds leave, they tell others about their experience, spreading the news of Jesus's arrival around town. Based on their testimony, I wonder how many curious people stop by to see baby Jesus.

As a result, Mary, Joseph, and Jesus could have seen a steady stream of visitors. Did any of these guests show up with food or gifts for the family? Since they're away from home and staying with farm animals, Mary and Joseph could certainly use any help they might receive.

When their baby is eight days old, it's time to circumcise him. They name him Jesus. This is what the angel told Joseph in his dream, and it aligns with what Gabriel told Mary when he appeared to her. It's significant that God independently told both Mary and Joseph the same thing: to name their son Jesus. This fact helps confirm for them that they both heard from God.

They go to the temple for the purification ceremony prescribed by Moses. There they consecrate the baby to God (Exodus 13:2) and offer a sacrifice (Exodus 13:12 and Leviticus 12:8). Though this seems most appropriate for Jesus, this isn't unique to him. This ceremony is prescribed for everyone by the law of Moses.

Since the temple is in Jerusalem and they're in Bethlehem, Mary and Joseph must travel there. The Bible doesn't say how long this journey takes them, but modern maps show these two towns to be about 5.5 miles (9 km) apart. Under normal conditions, this trip would take about two hours by foot. But remember, Mary has just given birth, so they will certainly go at a slower pace.

Again, we don't know if they travel by foot or if Mary has a donkey to ride. Regardless, she (or Joseph) holds baby Jesus the entire trip. Imagine clutching an eight-day-old baby, trying to keep him comfortable and not jostle him along the way. Traveling to the temple, as commanded by God, is not just a simple walk.

Questions*: How can we model Mary and Joseph's obedience to God? What is God telling us to do right now? Who can we help today by delivering a meal, offering a gift, or providing encouragement?*

Prayer: Heavenly Father, as we celebrate Jesus's first few days on earth, may we be mindful of what he came to do and who we are through him.

DECEMBER 28: MOVED BY THE SPIRIT

TODAY'S PASSAGE: LUKE 2:25–27

Focus verse: *It had been revealed to [Simeon] by the Holy Spirit that he would not die before he had seen the Lord's Messiah.* (Luke 2:26)

Jesus is now eight days old. Aside from his parents, only the shepherds really know who he is. Though others have surely seen him by now, they view him as nothing more than another baby, not God's promised Messiah.

This is about to change.

At the temple, two more people will see Jesus and embrace him for who he is. The first is Simeon.

Simeon is a righteous man. He's diligent about his relationship with the Lord. He obeys all the

Jewish laws set in place by Moses centuries earlier. Simeon knows what the prophecies foretell about the coming Savior. He believes that God will send the Messiah to save him and his people. Despite the fact that they have already waited centuries, Simeon expects that God will rescue them, just as the Scriptures promise.

Living with an any-day anticipation, the Holy Spirit reveals a shocking truth to Simeon. The Almighty confirms that this long-awaited Savior will arrive during Simeon's lifetime, promising the devoted man that he'll see Jesus before he dies.

Though many people lived their whole lives with the faith-filled expectancy of seeing the Savior, as promised by God, they died before he arrived. Simeon, however, believes God's promise that he'll see Jesus. It's just that God hasn't revealed when.

Then one day the Holy Spirit prompts Simeon to go to the temple courts. A wondering stirs within Simeon's soul. Will he see Jesus today?

Simeon obeys the Spirit's prompting. He goes to the temple and waits. We can imagine him arriving filled with anticipation, his heart thumping, and his pulse quickening as his eyes dart around, scanning all the people coming at the temple. *Which one is the Messiah?*

I suspect Simeon scrutinizes each adult male, wondering if the individual is God's chosen one. I doubt he gives teens, young children, or infants any consideration.

Then eight-day-old baby Jesus arrives at the temple with Mary and Joseph. They're there to fulfill the religious expectations that Moses decreed centuries earlier.

Though a baby is not likely what Simeon expected, the Holy Spirit confirms that this child is the One. He is the prophesied Savior, the Lord's Messiah.

Questions: *How well do we do at listening to the Holy Spirit's promptings? Do we obey without hesitation, first think before acting, or ignore what God reveals?*

Prayer: May we be open to hear you, Holy Spirit, when you speak. May we yield ourselves to your promptings and do what you tell us to do.

DECEMBER 29: A LIGHT TO THE GENTILES

TODAY'S PASSAGE: LUKE 2:28–32

Focus verse: *"For my eyes have seen your salvation, which you have prepared in the sight of all nations."* (Luke 2:30–31)

At the temple, Simeon walks up to Mary and Joseph. He takes baby Jesus from the new parents and holds the child in his arms. What must Mary and Joseph think? They don't know Simeon, but he interrupts the religious rite of circumcision they're about to go through, according to the Law of Moses (Leviticus 12:3). He interjects himself into their sacred moment as they prepare to consecrate Jesus to Father God.

Having a stranger pluck our newborn from our

arms would be disconcerting, but there's no mention of Mary or Joseph objecting or trying to stop Simeon. After all, shepherds showed up unannounced in the middle of the night to see Jesus. Maybe the actions of one man, in the temple, during the day, isn't so alarming in comparison.

While holding baby Jesus, Simeon praises the Lord.

The righteous man first thanks God for letting him see the Messiah, fulfilling the Almighty's promise to him. Through newborn Jesus, Simeon sees the salvation that will soon take place. He accepts it as fact, even though it won't occur for another three decades, well after he is gone.

Simeon affirms Jesus as the promised Savior for Israel—and for the entire world. But he switches the order from how the Old Testament normally presents it.

He first confirms that salvation is for all nations. It's a revelation to the Gentiles, that is, non-Jews. Then, after proclaiming Jesus as the light to the Gentiles, Simeon tacks on a final thought to his heavenward praise. He ends by noting that Jesus will also bring about glory for God's chosen people, Israel. Though Jesus, a Jew, came first for the Jews,

Simeon confirms that the Savior's broader and more significant mission is for everyone.

Now, having seen Jesus in person, Simeon's life is complete. He gives it over to God, knowing that he can now die in peace with the knowledge that Jesus has finally arrived.

After a lifetime of anticipation, God's promise has been fulfilled—and Simeon would have missed it had he ignored the Holy Spirit's prompting and stayed home that day.

Questions*: How can the fact that Jesus came first for his own people, the Jews, influence his non-Jewish followers today? What is a God-honoring attitude of Gentile Christians toward Jewish people today?*

Prayer: Lord, may we have your perspective toward your chosen people, the Jews, in all that we do. May we celebrate them as our spiritual ancestors.

DECEMBER 30: SIMEON'S MESSAGE FOR MARY

TODAY'S PASSAGE: LUKE 2:33–35

Focus verse: *"And a sword will pierce your own soul too."* (Luke 2:35)

S imeon's words of praise shock Joseph and Mary. Though God has already told them who their child is and what he will do, they may not yet fully understand the scope of Jesus's work and the impact he will have. Now Simeon has added more details.

It's a lot to take in. It's no wonder that they marvel at what he says.

This isn't a lack of faith on their part, just the reality that it requires repetition for something so radical, something so unprecedented, to make sense. Later in the Bible, we'll see Jesus's disciples struggle to fully grasp his mission—despite having spent three years with him.

After Simeon's prophetic praise to the Father, he blesses Mary, Joseph, and Jesus. Luke doesn't record this blessing for us, but he does tell us what else Simeon says. He focuses his attention on Mary and addresses her directly.

Simeon prophesies that Jesus will cause many people in the nation of Israel to fall and others to rise. Jesus will turn things upside down. Those on the religious inside—who think they're right with God—will fall, while others who may lack a religious pedigree will rise. The key is if they decide to follow Jesus, instead of following a bunch of rules and rituals.

Jesus will also bring controversy, with some speaking against him—opposing his ministry—which will reveal their true nature. This will serve as a sign to confirm him and who he is.

Everything, it seems, that Mary and Joseph have been taught about their faith will be transformed by Jesus.

Then Simeon gives Mary a personal prophecy. He says that a sword will pierce her soul too.

No parent hopes to outlive their children.

Having a child die stands as one of a parent's worst nightmares. But to watch a child suffer in one of the most gruesome executions ever conceived magnifies that pain to an unfathomable degree.

Just as a spear pierces Jesus's side physically on the cross, a sword will likewise pierce Mary's soul emotionally. She will suffer along with her son, as only a mother could.

Questions: *We don't have to suffer like Jesus did, but how well do we appreciate what he endured to save us? More importantly, do we follow Jesus or the many rules of his well-meaning followers?*

Prayer: Thank you, Jesus, for suffering in our place to pay the penalty our sins deserve, offering us forgiveness, and bringing us into a right relationship with Father God.

DECEMBER 31: ANNA'S TESTIMONY

TODAY'S PASSAGE: LUKE 2:36–38

Focus verse: *She gave thanks to God and spoke about the child to all who were looking forward to the redemption of Jerusalem.* (Luke 2:38)

A s Simeon concludes his praise, blessing, and prophecy, another witness arrives. Her name is Anna. Luke refers to her as the daughter of Penuel, from the tribe of Asher. She's also a widow—she had only been married for seven years when her husband died. That's all we know about her.

Some translations of the Bible say she's now eighty-four years old. Others say she's been a widow for eighty-four years. This would make her over one hundred. But either way she's old, *very* old as Luke writes.

While Luke applauds Simeon for his faith, he affirms Anna for her dedication. Both are noteworthy examples for us to follow.

Luke says that Anna never leaves the temple, worshiping God all day long and throughout the night. She spends all her time fasting and praying. This, of course, is an overstatement that Luke gives to emphasize her devout character. She can't always be at the temple, worshiping around the clock, and never eating or leaving to attend to other needs.

Luke exaggerates these characteristics to make a point. He wants to be sure we know Anna focuses her entire being on God. She's a devout woman who has dedicated her life to the Almighty, spending as much time as possible in the temple, fasting, praying, and worshiping.

That's dedication.

Spiritually, Anna spends her time with Father God. And now, Anna physically sees Jesus and spends time with him. She recognizes him as the promised Savior the prophets spoke of and that the people have been expecting for centuries.

Like Simeon, Anna praises God that she's lived long enough to see the Messiah, even though Jesus is an infant. And, like the shepherds eight days earlier, she shares her excitement with everyone.

After a lifetime of devotion to God, Anna receives an earthly reward by seeing Jesus. And her heavenly reward will be to live with him forever—along with the rest of his church (John 3:15).

Questions: *Like Anna, God invites us to focus on him, but do we? Though we no longer need to look forward to Jesus coming to save us, do we look forward to living with Jesus forever after we die?*

Prayer: Show us, Lord, how to live a life dedicated to you. May you receive all that we do as an act of worship. And may others see our words and actions as a witness that points them to you.

[Read about more people from Scripture in *The Friends and Foes of Jesus: Discover How People in the New Testament React to God's Good News.*]

JANUARY 1: GOING HOME

TODAY'S PASSAGE: LUKE 2:39

Focus verse: *They returned to Galilee to their own town of Nazareth.* (Luke 2:39)

A s we've covered, Mary and Joseph go to the temple in Jerusalem when Jesus is eight days old. They do so to consecrate him to God as their first-born male and to offer a sacrifice, both of which the law of Moses prescribes.

Yet Luke doesn't give us any details about either of these ceremonies.

Though consecrating Jesus to God seems like a significant event that we should hear about and celebrate, Luke doesn't tell us about Mary and Joseph making the required sacrifice. It's as if these two tasks don't matter.

What Luke focuses on, instead, are the conversations Mary and Joseph have with Simeon and Anna before they complete their reasons for going to the temple. The parents' interactions with these two godly individuals mean more. The words shared are more important than fulfilling the prescribed rituals.

After these two momentous conversations, Luke merely says that Mary and Joseph complete what the law requires. Then they return to their home in Nazareth.

This means they have more traveling to do.

It's about 90 miles (145 km) from Jerusalem to Nazareth. Under normal circumstances the trip would take four to five days to walk. But the circumstances for Mary, Joseph, and Jesus are not normal. During the journey to Bethlehem, Mary was in her final stages of pregnancy. This made the trip take longer.

Now they head home. That's another 90 miles. Though Mary is no longer pregnant, this trip is still challenging. Having just given birth, she's not in top physical condition. And attending to the needs of a newborn on this long journey adds difficulty to the trip.

Jesus requires frequent nursing as they travel. This means stopping along the way or trying to nurse while in transit. After each meal, the child has other physical needs to deal with.

Though Mary has the joy of a baby to lift her spirits as she travels, this doesn't make the trip less difficult for her to complete.

At last, they arrive home in Nazareth. Now they can begin to establish a normal life. Or so they think.

Questions: *Do we strive to live a normal life and get frustrated when God has other plans for us? When we must do something difficult for God, do we complain or embrace what we face?*

Prayer: Lord, keep us from letting what we think we're supposed to do get in the way of what you've planned for us. May we live the life you want us to, instead of the life we want.

[Read more about Luke's biography of Jesus in the Bible study *Dear Theophilus: A 40-Day Devotional Exploring the Life of Jesus through the Gospel of Luke.*]

JANUARY 2: ALIGNING LUKE'S AND MATTHEW'S TIMELINES

TODAY'S PASSAGE: MATTHEW 2:9–11

Focus verse: *On coming to the house, they saw the child with his mother Mary.* (Matthew 2:11)

During our journey toward Jesus's birth, we focused on the account in Luke. Joseph and his pregnant fiancé, Mary, travel from their home in Nazareth to Bethlehem for a mandatory census. While in Bethlehem, Mary gives birth to Jesus. Eight days later they go to the temple in Jerusalem to consecrate him and offer the required sacrifice. Then they head home for Nazareth.

Now we'll switch our discussion to the account in Matthew. Here's a summary of his version:

Matthew's first mention of a location is Bethlehem, where Jesus is born. Then he talks about Magi, which no other biblical writer mentions. The Magi first spot a star and follow its path to Jerusalem—the area's religious center and home to King Herod—seeking the newborn King. He's not there.

Herod receives the Magi and consults with the religious scholars, who say the promised Messiah will be born in Bethlehem, only a few miles away. Herod tells the Magi to seek the child and report back. They head out and follow the star until they find Jesus. He's in a house, no longer lying in a manger. They give him gifts and return home by a different route. God then tells Joseph in a dream to flee to Egypt so that Herod can't kill Jesus.

At first glance, the two accounts don't align well. But this is because of some false assumptions.

First, we assume, like Herod, that the sign the Magi see first appeared when Jesus was born. In fact, God could have caused the sign to appear well before that, giving them time to arrive shortly after Jesus's birth.

The second assumption is that the Magi find Jesus in Bethlehem, but the Bible doesn't say that. It says they search for him, using the star to guide them, and eventually find him.

Third, some Bible scholars suggest the Magi arrive two years after Jesus is born. They propose this based on Herod's decree to kill all babies in Bethlehem up to two years old. But it's easy to see Herod, a megalomaniac, taking the Magi's report, rounding it up to one year, and then doubling it to make sure.

Setting these assumptions aside, here's an alternate way to see the timeline unfold:

Jesus is born in Bethlehem as Luke and Matthew say. The Magi, having begun their journey months earlier, arrive in Jerusalem about the same time as his birth. They search for him in Bethlehem but don't find him. This is because Mary, Joseph, and Jesus have already gone to Jerusalem before heading home to Nazareth.

The Magi notice that the position of the star has shifted. They follow it to a new location. It stops over Nazareth, and they find baby Jesus in his parents' house.

This, of course, is speculation, but it does allow the two accounts to align nicely and is the perspective we'll follow.

When some people see things in Scripture that

don't make sense, their response—the wrong response—can be to reject the Bible as flawed. Then they reject Jesus.

When we read passages in the Bible that confuse us, the better reaction is to recognize that we are finite people who will never fully grasp the complexities of our infinite Creator who is all-powerful and all-knowing.

From this perspective, we can move forward with confidence to meditate on these confusing passages and ask for clarity through Holy Spirit insight. In some cases, God gives the insight we look for. In other cases, the answer still evades us. When this happens, we can embrace these passages as a delightful mystery and then praise God anyway.

Questions: *What do we do when we face passages in the Bible we don't understand? How content are we to accept some things about God as a mystery?*

Prayer: God, give us your perspective to understand your Word and the peace to accept what is beyond our comprehension.

JANUARY 3: THE KING OF THE JEWS
TODAY'S PASSAGE: MATTHEW 2:1–2

Focus verse: *"Where is the one who has been born king of the Jews?"* (Matthew 2:2)

N ow let's focus on the Magi who come to visit Jesus. Matthew is the only writer in Scripture who mentions them.

First, we must dispel some common misconceptions that come to us from the classic Christmas carol "We Three Kings" (also known as "We Three Kings of Orient Are"). The opening line of the song calls them kings, says there are three, and says they traveled from the Orient. Though we don't want to altogether dismiss this beloved song, we must acknowledge that none of these facts are biblical.

Scripture says that the Magi, also called wisemen or astrologers in various translations, come from the East in search of Jesus. It doesn't say how many Magi there are, but it does say that as a group they bring three gifts. Though they could have come from the Orient, they more likely hail from Persia. Either way, they have traveled a long distance to find Jesus.

The Magi's interest in Jesus, the King of the Jews, is perplexing.

Their explanation is simply that they saw a new star in the sky and came to worship the birth of the king that the star represented. It's easy to see these wise men studying the stars in the night skies and noticing one they'd never seen before. We can assume they either follow a commonly held assumption or they search ancient texts to conclude the new star represents the birth of the king.

There's no hint in Matthew's text that they have any Jewish connection or even any knowledge of the God revealed in Scripture. Yet they set out on a long journey in complete faith that a king has been born—a king of great significance. They intend to find him, worship him, and give him gifts.

As they follow the star, they reach Jerusalem, the political and religious center of the area. They seek out King Herod, likely reasoning that the baby—the King of the Jews—is his. Or at least he would know where they can find the child. But it turns out the Magi have made a false assumption about where to find Jesus.

Questions: *What false assumptions might we hold about Jesus? How can we embrace Jesus as the King of the Jews and the Savior of everyone else too?*

Prayer: Father, show us how we can pursue Jesus with the same passion as the Magi. May we find him, worship him, and give him our gifts.

JANUARY 4: SEARCHING FOR JESUS

TODAY'S PASSAGE: MATTHEW 2:3–8

Focus verse: *"Go and search carefully for the child."*
(Matthew 2:8)

The Magi's question about a king being born disturbs Herod. This event is news to him, and it isn't good news. This unknown child who will become king threatens Herod's rule and the power he has amassed.

Since Herod is concerned about this revelation, so is everyone else in Jerusalem. It's in their best interest to align their thoughts with his, to worry about what worries him and celebrate what he celebrates. Whether good or bad, what matters to Herod affects them too.

Yet other people surely feel silent excitement about the birth of the King of the Jews, wondering if he's the promised Savior foretold by the Scriptures.

Herod demands answers about this so-called king. He seeks the religious scholars to learn where the Scriptures prophesy the Messiah will be born. They have an answer: he will be born in Bethlehem, in the territory of Judah (Micah 5:2).

King David, we may recall, came from the tribe of Judah (1 Samuel 17:12). And the Savior will come from his royal line, his descendants (2 Samuel 7:16). Everything aligns.

Armed with this newfound information—that the Messiah will be born in Bethlehem—Herod has a secret meeting with the Magi. He asks them when the star first appeared, assuming it was birthed the same time as the Messiah. He doesn't make this request out of mere curiosity; he's already scheming what he'll do to stop this child who threatens his reign.

Since Herod wants to discover the whereabouts of this child, he instructs the Magi to go to Bethlehem and search for the newborn who will become king. Then he tells them to report back on the baby's location. He feigns interest in wanting to go and worship the boy too.

It's interesting that the Magi, who come from a foreign culture and a distant land, want to find Jesus and worship him. Yet Herod, who should be excited about the arrival of the King of the Jews, is troubled by his existence and wants to kill him.

Questions: *Do we pretend, like Herod, to have a fascination with Jesus and a desire to worship him, or is our interest in Jesus genuine? How well do we follow Jesus as our King?*

Prayer: Jesus, when we search for you, may we find you. Let what we read about you in the Bible draw us closer to you.

JANUARY 5: WORSHIPING JESUS

TODAY'S PASSAGE: MATTHEW 2:9–12

Focus verse: *They bowed down and worshiped him.*
(Matthew 2:11)

After Herod's meeting with the Magi, they head out to search for Jesus. They've been told to look in Bethlehem, which is only a few miles away. Yet the Bible doesn't say the Magi find Jesus in Bethlehem.

What the Bible does say is that they follow the star as it moves ahead of them. It doesn't seem they'd need a light in the sky to direct them on a five-mile trip to Bethlehem, but a guiding star would be instrumental in redirecting their course 90 miles north to the city of Nazareth.

Remember, the chronology we're using is that Jesus is born in Bethlehem, eight days later he and his parents go to Jerusalem, and then they return home to Nazareth, which would take about four days.

As a result, they arrive home about twelve days after Jesus's birth, which is the traditional time when the Magi arrive, as celebrated by Epiphany. This means that the Magi discover Jesus and his parents in their home in Nazareth when he's twelve days old.

Regardless of the specifics, when the star stops moving, the Magi know they're close. They're over-joyed. They come to the house and see Jesus with his mother. Then they bow down and worship him.

What must Mary think, having a group of strangers arrive and bow down to worship her baby? Yes, she's seen many extraordinary things since Gabriel first came to her nine months earlier, but this is noteworthy. These aren't poor, nearby shepherds arriving out of curiosity; these are wealthy men who traveled a long distance to bow before her son.

They've also brought treasures to give to him. They present Jesus with gold, frankincense, and myrrh. These are gifts worthy of a king. And they rightly perceive him to be a king.

Having completed their mission of worshiping Jesus and giving him their gifts, God warns the Magi in a dream to not report back to King Herod. Instead, they go home by a different route.

Questions: *What gifts do we give to Jesus? How can the ways we follow and serve Jesus be offered to him as a gift?*

Prayer: Jesus, may you accept all that we do and say as a gift to you. Receive our actions as our sincere worship.

JANUARY 6: FLEEING FROM HEROD
TODAY'S PASSAGE: MATTHEW 2:13–18

Focus verse: *"Get up," [the angel] said, "take the child and his mother and escape to Egypt."* (Matthew 2:13)

Mary and Joseph have just arrived back at their home in Nazareth. They may have assumed that now they can settle down and their life will return to normal. They're wrong.

Magi showed up, possibly on the same day Mary, Joseph, and Jesus returned home. These men condescended themselves, bowing before Jesus and giving him gifts fit for a king. Then they left.

That night, on the evening of Epiphany, God sends his angel to Joseph in a dream. The angel tells

Joseph to get up and flee with Jesus and Mary to Egypt. Herod is going to search for Jesus with the intent to kill him. They're to stay in this foreign land until Joseph hears differently.

Joseph has experienced receiving supernatural instructions before. The first time was when the angel appeared to him in a dream and told him that his fiancée's pregnancy came through the Holy Spirit and to take her as his wife. Joseph obeyed the angel's first instructions, and he obeys again this time.

Joseph gets up and leaves with Mary and Jesus that night, heading for Egypt. I doubt they dare risk saying goodbye to their family and friends or even tell anyone where they're headed.

After all, if the Magi could find them in Nazareth, what's to keep Herod from also locating them? He could start in Bethlehem as the prophecy foretold. Many people there know about Jesus because the shepherds told everyone what happened. It wouldn't be hard to trace Jesus from there to Jerusalem eight days later. And people at the temple know about him because Anna also spread the word. From there, someone must've seen them head off for Nazareth. But if no one in

Nazareth knows where they went, Herod's search ends there.

Yet how painful it must be for Mary and Joseph to leave their hometown without saying goodbye to family and friends, not knowing when—or if—they might return.

This, however, will fulfill the prophecy in Hosea 11:1 which says that God will call his son out of Egypt.

For his part, Herod is furious when the Magi don't report back on Jesus's whereabouts. The king orders the death of all baby boys in and around Bethlehem who are less than two years old (Matthew 2:16–18, which quotes Jerimiah 31:15).

Yet God spares Jesus from Herod's widespread execution order and a premature death. God's plan is for Jesus to die on the cross in payment for the sins of everyone, not at the hands of a paranoid ruler before Jesus can complete his mission.

Living safely in Egypt for a time protects Jesus so he can later fulfill his mission to save all of humanity, just as God planned and the prophets in the Old Testament foretold.

Questions: *When has God told us to do something extreme? How well do we obey God's directions?*

Prayer: Father God, thank you for saving Jesus from the clutches of Herod so that Jesus could later die to save us. And Jesus, thank you for coming to earth to serve as the ultimate sacrifice to end all sacrifices.

EPILOGUE: JESUS'S EARLY LIFE

TODAY'S PASSAGE: LUKE 2:40–52

Focus verse: *Jesus grew in wisdom and stature, and in favor with God and man.* (Luke 2:52)

Matthew doesn't say how long Jesus and his parents stay in Egypt, but when it's time to come back an angel appears to Joseph in a dream. This is the third significant nighttime revelation for Joseph. The first supernatural dream was an angel telling him about Mary's pregnancy and to marry her anyway. The second time occurred nine months later with the instruction to flee to Egypt.

This time the angel says it's safe to return to

their home country, to get up and take his family back to Israel. Joseph does.

He considers going to the region of Judea, where Jesus was born (Bethlehem is in Judea). But an angel comes to him a fourth time in a dream, warning him to not go there. Joseph obeys and takes his family to Nazareth, in the region of Galilee (Matthew 2:19–23).

Now we return to Luke's account of Jesus to continue our story.

Luke simply says that after Mary and Joseph return to Nazareth, Jesus grows and becomes strong. Wisdom fills him, and God's grace is on him.

Father God's hand is upon Jesus. Yet don't infer that Jesus's childhood is different than any other child's. He also needs his earthly parents to raise him, teaching him and guiding him as he grows into manhood. I'm sure he gets into his own share of mischief and squabbles with his younger siblings. He, at times, even perplexes his parents and causes them to worry.

The Bible only gives us one story of Jesus's youth. In this account we see the balance between his divine nature and his human side. The incident occurs when he's twelve.

Jesus goes with his parents to celebrate the Passover in Jerusalem. When the festival ends, his parents head for home, traveling with a large group of family, friends, and other sojourners headed in the same direction. They assume Jesus is with the caravan. But he isn't. He stays behind without their knowledge or their approval.

After traveling all day, Mary and Joseph discover that Jesus isn't in the convoy. They've lost their son, one of a parent's most dreaded nightmares. Yet for them it's even worse. They've also lost the Son of God.

Panicked, they head back to Jerusalem. Luke doesn't say if they wait until morning or leave at once, traveling throughout the night to arrive there by dawn. Either way, they don't find him right away. They search. And they search. After three days they finally find him.

He's in the temple having a deep spiritual conversation with the teachers. He listens to what they say and asks insightful questions. Everyone is amazed at the twelve-year-old's depth of understanding. His parents are astonished too.

Yet they're also irritated with him for causing them needless worry.

Young Jesus responds incredulously. "Why were you searching for me? Didn't you know I had to be in my Father's house?" (Luke 2:49–50). These are the first recorded words of Jesus.

His parents don't understand what he means, but Jesus obediently returns home with them. He grows in wisdom and stature, enjoying the favor of both God and men. This prepares him for ministry, which he'll start in eighteen years, when he's thirty years old.

That ministry is why he came to earth. This is the reason we celebrate the Advent of Jesus.

Questions: *What should we do now to prepare us for what God has planned for our future? When people look for us, where will they find us?*

Prayer: Lord, bless us, that we may grow in wisdom and stature. Prepare us for what lies ahead. May we find favor with both you and others.

If you liked *The Advent of Jesus*, please leave a review online. Your review will help others discover this book and encourage them to read it too.

Thank you.

HOLIDAY CELEBRATION DEVOTIONALS

Which devotional do you want to read next?

- The Passion of Jesus (Lent)
- The Victory of Jesus (Easter)
- The Ministry of Jesus
- Thanksgiving with Jesus
- New Year with Jesus

Be the first to hear about Peter's new books and receive updates at PeterDeHaan.com/updates.

IF YOU'RE NEW TO THE BIBLE

Each entry in this book contains Bible references. These can guide you if you want to learn more. If you're not familiar with the Bible, here's an overview to get you started, give some context, and minimize confusion.

First, the Bible is a collection of works written by various authors over several centuries. Think of the Bible as a diverse anthology of godly communication. It contains historical accounts, poetry, songs, letters of instruction and encouragement, messages from God sent through his representatives, and prophecies.

Most versions of the Bible have sixty-six books grouped into two sections: The Old Testament and the New Testament. The Old Testament contains thirty-nine books that precede and anticipate Jesus. The New Testament includes twenty-seven books and covers Jesus's life and the work of his followers.

The reference notations in the Bible, such as Romans 3:23, are analogous to line numbers in a Shakespearean play. They serve as a study aid. Since the Bible is much longer and more complex than a play, its reference notations are more involved.

As already mentioned, the Bible is an amalgam of books, or sections, such as Genesis, Matthew, or Acts. These are the names given to them, over time, based on the piece's author, audience, or purpose.

In the 1200s, each book was divided into chapters, such as Acts 2 or Psalm 23. In the 1500s, the chapters were further subdivided into verses, such as John 3:16. Let's use this as an example.

The name of the book (John) appears first, followed by the chapter number (3), a colon, and then the verse number (16). Sometimes called a chapter-verse reference notation, this helps people quickly find a specific text regardless of their version of the Bible.

Although the goal was to place these chapter and verse divisions at logical breaks, they sometimes seem arbitrary. Therefore, it's good practice to read what precedes and follows each passage you're studying. The text before or after it may contain relevant insights into the portion you're exploring.

Here's how to look up a specific passage in the Bible based on its reference: Most Bibles contain a table of contents, which gives the page number for the beginning of each book. Start there. Locate the book you want to read, and turn to that page. Then flip forward to the chapter you want. Last, skim that chapter to locate the specific verse.

If you want to read online, enter the reference into BibleGateway.com or BibleHub.com. Also check out the YouVersion app.

Learn more about the greatest book ever written at ABibleADay.com, which provides a Bible blog, summaries of the books of the Bible, a dictionary of Bible terms, Bible reading plans, and other resources.

ABOUT PETER DEHAAN

Peter DeHaan, PhD, wants to change the world one word at a time. His books and blog posts discuss God, the Bible, and church, geared toward spiritual seekers and church dropouts. Many people feel church has let them down, and Peter seeks to encourage them as they search for a place to belong.

But he's not afraid to ask tough questions or make religious people squirm. He's not trying to be provocative. Instead, he seeks truth, even if it makes people uncomfortable. Peter urges Christians to push past the status quo and reexamine how they practice their faith in every part of their lives.

Peter earned his doctorate, awarded with high distinction, from Trinity College of the Bible and Theological Seminary. He lives with his wife in beautiful Southwest Michigan and wrangles crossword puzzles in his spare time.

A lifelong student of Scripture, Peter wrote the 1,000-page website ABibleADay.com to encourage people to explore the Bible, the greatest book ever written. His popular blog addresses biblical Christianity to build a faith that matters.

Read his blog, receive his newsletter, and learn more at PeterDeHaan.com.

BOOKS BY PETER DEHAAN

Holiday Celebration Devotionals

The Advent of Jesus

The Passion of Jesus (Lent)

The Victory of Jesus (Easter)

The Ministry of Jesus

Thanksgiving with Jesus

New Year with Jesus

40-Day Bible Study Series

Dear Theophilus (the Gospel of Luke)

Acts Bible Study

Isaiah Bible Study

Minor Prophets Bible Study

Job Bible Study

Living Water (John)

Love Is Patient (1 and 2 Corinthians)

Revelation Bible Study

1, 2, & 3 John Bible Study

Hebrews Bible Study

James and Jude Bible Study

Matthew Bible Study

1 & 2 Peter Bible Study

Mark Bible Study

Bible Character Sketches Series

Women of the Bible

The Friends and Foes of Jesus

Old Testament Sinners and Saints

More Old Testament Sinners and Saints

Heroes and Heavies of the Apocrypha

200 Old Testament Sinners and Saints

Visiting Churches Series

52 Churches

The 52 Churches Workbook

More Than 52 Churches

The More Than 52 Churches Workbook

Visiting Online Church

Other Books

Elephant God

Jesus's Broken Church

Martin Luther's 95 Theses

The Christian Church's LGBTQ Failure

Bridging the Sacred-Secular Divide (formerly *Woodpecker Wars*)

Beyond Psalm 150

How Big Is Your Tent?

For the latest list of all Peter's books, go to PeterDeHaan.com/books.